*Publications of the*

CENTRE FOR REFORMATION AND RENAISSANCE STUDIES

Renaissance and Reformation Texts in Translation, 8

SERIES EDITOR John McClelland

Victoria University
in the
University of Toronto

# Romeo and Juliet before Shakespeare

## *Four Early Stories of Star-Crossed Love*

by

Masuccio Salernitano, Luigi da Porto, Matteo Bandello, and Pierre Boaistuau

Translated, with an Introduction and Notes, by

Nicole Prunster

Toronto

Centre for Reformation and Renaissance Studies

2000

CRRS Publications
Centre for Reformation and Renaissance Studies
Victoria University in the University of Toronto
Toronto, Canada M5S 1K7


Printed in Canada

**Canadian Cataloguing in Publication Data**

Main entry under title:

Romeo and Juliet before Shakespeare: four early stories of star-crossed love

(Renaissance and Reformation texts in translation, ISSN 0820-750X ; 8)
Contents: Mariotto and Ganozza / Masuccio Salernitano – A tale about two noble lovers / Luigi da Porto – The unfortunate death of two most wretched lovers / Matteo Bandello – Of two lovers / Pierre Boaistuau.
Includes bibliographical references.
ISBN 0-7727-2015-0

1. Italian fiction – 15th century – Translations into English. 2. Italian fiction – 16th century – Translations into English. 3. Shakepeare, William, 1564–1616. Romeo and Juliet – Sources. I. Prunster, N. (Nicole), 1945– . II. Victoria University (Toronto, Ont.) Centre for Reformation and Renaissance Studies. III. Series.

PQ4253.A5R65 2000 853′.308 C00-930994-2



Cover illustration: Anon., *Storia di Uberto e Filomena,* XV cent.

Cover design: Ian MacKenzie, Paragraphics

Typesetting and printing: Becker Associates

For my father, Ron, who started me on this path.
With love.

# *Preface*

Shakespeare did not invent the story of Romeo and Juliet out of whole cloth. Many versions of the tale, both continental and English, circulated during the fifteenth and sixteenth centuries, and he had ready access to some of them. The present volume contains four of these versions, three Italian and one French, in translation into modern English. They have been selected because they constitute the main stream, as it were, of the story's evolution toward the tragedy's definitive literary realisation. The reader is invited to compare them among themselves and with Shakespeare's play.

I wish to express my sincere thanks to Jean Gassin and to my colleague Tony Pagliaro, who taught me a valuable lesson on linguistic registers. I am also grateful to the La Trobe University Publications Committee for its financial support, and to John McClelland and the readers of the Publications Committee of the Centre for Reformation and Renaissance Studies for their sound advice and boundless patience.

Nicole Prunster

The publishers wish to thank the Hambledon Press for kind permission to reproduce the maps of Verona on pp. 12–13 from *War, Culture and Society in Renaissance Venice.*

**This publication has been supported by La Trobe University**
**Internet: http://www.latrobe.edu.au**

*Contents*

# *Introduction*

## 1. The Authors

### i) *Masuccio Salernitano (circa 1410–1475)*

Although known as Masuccio Salernitano, the author of the *Novellino* was born Tommaso Guardati into a noble family from Salerno. It was here that he spent his youth and carried out his somewhat irregular studies, which included the works of Dante and Boccaccio and sufficient Latin to allow him to enter public office. As Masuccio frequented court circles both in Salerno and Naples, he became known to King Ferdinand, to the Duke of Calabria and to the wife of the latter, Ippolita Maria Visconti. It was here also that he became acquainted with many of the leading writers and intellectuals of the Aragonese court, including Giovanni Pontano. Shortly after 1463 Masuccio became secretary to Roberto Sanseverino, the Prince of Salerno, whom he served until Sanseverino's death in 1474.

Masuccio himself died before he could complete the definitive version of his sole literary work, the *Novellino*, a collection of fifty novellas published the year following his death by his friend Francesco del Tuppo, a Neapolitan writer and publisher, in collaboration with another publisher, Sisto Riessinger. As this *editio princeps* has been lost, the earliest surviving edition is that published in Milan in 1483.

Although in writing his *Novellino* Masuccio was clearly influenced by the *Decameron* (1349–1353) of Giovanni Boccaccio, there is much that distinguishes the later work from the one hundred tales comprising Boccaccio's masterpiece. The tone of the *Novellino* is, for instance, often bitingly satiric and polemical, and never more so than when the author presents the shortcomings of the clergy and women, with the result that Masuccio the moralist/misogynist at times has the better of Masuccio the artist. Comic novellas alternate with others in which a predilection for the horrific and gruesome is apparent as the author strives to present humanity in all its many and contradictory manifestations.

The language of the *Novellino* further distinguishes it from Boccaccio's *Decameron* which, early in the sixteenth century, was to become the model *par excellence* for prose writers, both where language and content were concerned. Masuccio, in his efforts at constructing a noble literary language, has frequent and deliberate recourse to both dialect elements and archaic terms.

In its structure, also, the *Novellino* differs from that of the Boccaccian archetype with its narrative frame within which the one hundred tales are narrated over ten days, eight of which have a theme that the storytellers (with the exception of the rebellious Dioneo) must illustrate as they entertain their companions with their individual tales. The *Novellino* instead is divided into five parts each consisting of ten novellas illustrating five separate themes: the misdeeds of the clergy; tricks and injuries caused by jealousy; the "defective" female sex; tales with happy and unhappy endings; tales dealing with the magnanimity of princes. Each novella is preceded by a brief summary (the "argomento") and a dedication ("esordio") to a member of the Aragonese court. Following the tale itself (the "narrazione") there is the author's reflection on it which bears his own name ("Masuccio"). The work as a whole is prefaced by a dedication to the Duchess of Calabria, Ippolita of Aragon, and concludes with the author addressing his own work and recalling his former patron, Roberto Sanseverino, Prince of Salerno.

### ii) *Luigi da Porto (1485–1529)*

Born in Vicenza in 1485, Luigi da Porto was entrusted firstly to the tutelage of his grandfather following the premature deaths of his parents and then (in 1493) to that of his maternal uncle, Francesco Savorgnan. From 1505 he frequented the cultured circles of Vicenza, and it was during this period that he began corresponding with the eminent Venetian poet and literary theorist, Pietro Bembo, and made the acquaintance of Matteo Bandello.

After the war of the League of Cambrai broke out in 1509, Da Porto described in his letters Friuli invaded by Imperial troups, the siege of Padua and the entry of the Emperor Maximilian I into Vicenza on 25 October of that year.[1] A month later he was a soldier in the Venetian army when it recaptured Vicenza. Da Porto was gravely wounded in the throat in 1511, a wound from which he never fully recovered. He remained in Venice until 1517, when once more Vicenza was wrested from the Imperial army by Venetian troups.

During the latter part of his life Da Porto devoted himself to organising his seventy letters, written principally to his uncle when he was a soldier during the war of the League of Cambrai (1509–1511) and then in the years immediately following his wounding. In his later years he also wrote some seventy-three poems, mainly Petrarchan sonnets, which were first published in Venice in 1539, together with the modified version of his novella, with the title *Rime et Prosa di M. Luigi da Porto*. This volume, edited by Da Porto's brother Bernardino and published by Francesco Marcolini, is dedicated to Pietro Bembo.

Da Porto wrote his novella in 1524, as is attested by an appreciative letter which Bembo wrote to him in June of the same year. In this letter Bembo praises highly Da Porto's novella, the manuscript of which the author had evidently sent to him. First published in Venice by Benedetto de Bendoni, probably in 1531, with the long title "Hystoria novellamente ritrovata di due nobili amanti, con la loro pietosa morte, intervenuta già nella città di Verona nel tempo del Signor Bartolomeo dalla Scala", Da Porto's tale was subsequently reprinted by Bendoni's brother Bernardino in 1535. In the 1539 Marcolini edition, the modified tale is entitled simply *La Giulietta*. Both versions are preceded by the author's dedication to Lucina Savorgnana, in which he explains how he himself supposedly came to hear the tale of the two Veronese lovers. As the 1539 Marcolini edition is dedicated to Bembo, it is feasible to assume that the modifications in it may be due to suggestions which he had made to Da Porto after reading the manuscript. Bembo's friendship and respect for the author are evidenced by the sincere grief he expresses in a letter to Bernardino following his brother Luigi's death on 10 May 1529.

### iii) *Matteo Bandello (1485–1561)*

Born in Castelnuovo Scrivia in Lombardy, Bandello received his religious and literary education in the Milanese convent of Santa Maria delle Grazie where his uncle Vincenzo was prior. After further studies at the University of Pavia, Bandello himself became a Dominican friar early in the sixteenth century and journeyed throughout France and central and southern Italy with his uncle who by then had become general of the Dominican order. Following the death of Vincenzo in 1506 Bandello returned to Milan and began frequenting the aristocratic salons of Lombardy, including that of Ippolita Sforza Bentivoglio.

From 1508 Bandello held diplomatic posts in the courts of Milan and Mantua but was forced to flee his home in 1525 when Spanish troops took over Lombardy following the battle of Pavia. Having abandoned the Dominican order, he served such eminent figures as Francesco Gonzaga, Giovanni delle Bande Nere, and the Genoese exile Cesare Fregoso, mercenary captain in the employ of the Venetian Republic. After the Emperor Charles V had had Fregoso killed in 1541, Bandello accompanied his widow, Costanza Rangone, to France where King Henry II made him bishop of Agen, a post he held until his death in 1561.

Bandello's minor works include *Le tre Parche* (1531), a poem in *terza rima* in honour of the first son of Fregoso and his wife Costanza; the *Canti XI* (1536–1538), a poem in *ottava rima* in praise of Lucrezia Gonzaga; a collection of Petrarchan verse entitled *Alcuni fragmenti de le rime* (1554) and dedicated to Marguerite de Navarre, sister of King Francis I of France and herself the author of the *Heptaméron*, a collection of novellas; a Latin version of Boccaccio's tale of Tito and Gisippo (*Decameron* X,8); a vernacular version of Euripides' *Hecuba* (1539); a Latin biography of the Genoese friar Giambattista Cattaneo (1504); and a collection of letters.

Bandello's major literary work is his collection of 214 novellas, begun in his youth at the urging of Ippolita Sforza Bentivoglio and completed late in his life. The tales are divided into four parts, the first three of which were published by Vincenzo Busdrago in Lucca in 1554, the last, posthumously, by Alessandro Marsilii in Lyons in 1573. As Da Porto does with his tale, Bandello prefaces each of his with a dedicatory letter in which he recalls (or pretends to recall) the circumstances in which he himself heard the tale before committing it to paper; and in common with Masuccio Salernitano, he does not attempt to imitate the language of the *Decameron*, instead openly declaring himself Lombard in the preface to the first of the four parts ("Il Bandello ai candidi e umani lettori"). Unlike Boccaccio and Masuccio, however, Bandello does not group his novellas according to their content.

Three of Shakespeare's dramas—*Romeo and Juliet* (1596), *Much Ado About Nothing* (1598), *Twelfth Night* (1600)—and John

Webster's *The Duchess of Malfi* (first production circa 1613) are based on Bandello novellas which the English dramatists knew through the French versions of Pierre Boaistuau and François de Belleforest.

## iv) *Pierre Boaistuau (circa 1517–1566)*

What little is known of Boaistuau must be deduced largely from the unreliable testimony which he gives about himself in his own works. Born into the lower middle class of Nantes around 1517, between 1543 and 1550 Boaistuau attended the Universities of Poitiers, Valence, and Avignon, where he claims to have studied civil and canon law. In Rome he associated with doctors, which stimulated his interest in the extraordinary and exceptional, an interest which he further pursued upon returning to Paris where, from 1550, he resumed his scientific research.

Not content merely to observe the marvels of nature, Boaistuau attempted also to understand and reproduce them. Thus he sought to create precious stones and investigated the secret properties of plants and of human beings. This led him to dissecting rooms in his efforts at understanding the causes of death. Around 1554 Boaistuau became secretary to Jean-Jacques de Cambrai, French ambassador to the Levant, and subsequently traveled with him throughout Europe.

Boaistuau's first literary work, the little-known *Histoire de Chelidonius Tigurinus, sur l'Institution des Princes Chrestiens, & origine des Royaumes*, in the tradition of the "miroir du prince", was published in Paris in 1556. 1558 saw the publication of both *Le théâtre du monde* (belonging to the genre "miseria hominis") and his *Bref discours de l'excellence & dignité de l'homme*, which deal respectively with the suffering which accompanies those who exclude God from their lives, and the dignity which elevates those who are instead mindful of their divine origins and hence follow God's word.

In the latter part of 1558 Boaistuau published in Paris a third work, entitled *Histoires des amans fortunez*, which is in fact the first edition of the novellas of Marguerite de Navarre. Boaistuau's version contains only sixty-seven of the seventy-two tales, places them in a different order from the one intended, introduces unauthorised amendments and corrections, and omits the name of the real author. These transgressions were subsequently rectified in the 1559 edition by Claude Gruget, retitled the *Heptaméron*.

The year 1559 also saw the publication of Boaistuau's *Histoires tragiques*, adaptations into French of six Bandello novellas. At the end of this same year, Boaistuau left for England with a special edition of this work, dedicated to the young Queen Elizabeth, in which all disparaging references to the British monarchy had been judiciously suppressed, and a significant modification made to the title page as well. Whereas in the *editio princeps* (Paris: Vincent Sertenas, 1559) it is specified that Boaistuau's *Histoires tragiques* derive from the "oeuvres italiennes de Bandel" [the Italian works of Bandello], on the title page of the edition dedicated to Elizabeth I (Paris: n.p., 1559) Boaistuau acknowledges vaguely "quelques fameux autheurs, Italiens & Latins" [some famous Italian and Latin authors] as his source. Boaistuau's dubious ethics notwithstanding, the twenty-one editions of the *Histoires tragiques* in the space of some fifty years testify to the work's popularity; and between 1559 and 1582 his collaborator François de Belleforest added significantly to the number of translations of Bandello novellas that Boaistuau had earlier undertaken.

## 2. The evolution of the Romeo and Juliet tale

Few stories have aroused as much critical attention or have proved as adaptable to different genres as that dealing with the chivalrous but ill-fated love of Romeo and Juliet at odds with a hostile and materialistically-oriented society. Scholars seeking to determine the origins of Shakespeare's drama are in general agreement that the principal line of development in Italy begins with the thirty-third novella of Masuccio Salernitano's *Novellino*, first published in 1476, which deals with the vicissitudes of two Sienese lovers, Mariotto and Ganozza. In his seminal study of the Romeo and Juliet legend prior to Shakespeare's drama, Olin H. Moore suggests that Masuccio draws upon two principal sources for his novella: the fifteenth-century tale "Istorietta amorosa fra Leonora de' Bardi e Ippolito Bondelmonti" and Boccaccio's *Decameron*, predominantly III,8 and X,4.[2] Masuccio's novella is subsequently elaborated by Luigi da Porto in his considerably longer version, first published in Venice around 1530, and bearing the title/summary "Istoria novellamente ritrovata di due nobili amanti con la loro pietosa morte, intervenuta già nella città di Verona nel tempo del signor Bartolomeo dalla Scala". Da Porto's contribution to the development of the tale is considerable:

it is in his version that the lovers are renamed Giulietta and Romeo and are members of two eminent, historical families, the Cappelletti and the Montecchi, engaged in a bloody feud in Verona during the rule of Bartolomeo della Scala.

Adaptations of Da Porto's novella were not slow to appear. In the preface to his translation of Boccaccio's *Filocolo*, published in Paris in 1542, Adrien Sevin included a tale transparently indebted to Da Porto's, despite the pseudo-Greek setting and names of the characters. In Italy, a poem in *ottava rima* by Gerardo (or Gherardo) Boldieri, published in 1553 under the pseudonym Clizia, also draws significantly on Da Porto's tale while introducing several innovations. The following year saw the publication in Lucca of Matteo Bandello's novella "La sfortunata morte di dui infelicissimi amanti che l'uno di veleno e l'altro di dolore morirono, con vari accidenti", the ninth tale of the second part of his *Novelle*, derived also from Da Porto with borrowings both from the "Istorietta amorosa fra Leonora de' Bardi e Ippolito Bondelmonti" and from Clizia's poem. This (together with five other Bandello novellas) was subsequently translated/adapted into French by Pierre Boaistuau in 1559. In 1578, Luigi Groto contributed to the evolutionary mosaic by writing *La Hadriana*, a tragedy in blank verse reprinted nine times between 1582 and 1626. Despite the change in setting and in the names of the characters, Groto appears to have been influenced by the earlier versions of the tale, including that by Boaistuau. It has been suggested that Shakespeare may have known Groto's tragedy, or that both poets had access to a lost source.[3] Spain's Golden Age playwright and poet, Lope Félix de Vega Carpio, was also susceptible early in his career to the Romeo and Juliet story: his tragicomedy *Castelvines y Monteses* was written around 1608.[4]

What seems indisputable in the evolutionary line which leads from Masuccio to Shakespeare is the intermediary role played by Pierre Boaistuau's "Histoire troisiesme de deux amans, dont l'un mourut de venin, l'autre de tristesse", closely based as it is on Bandello's tale and adapted in turn by Arthur Brooke in his long poem, "The Tragicall Historye of Romeus and Juliet"[5] (1562) and by William Painter in a prose translation appearing in the second volume of his *Palace of Pleasure* (1567). It is believed that Shakespeare knew both versions, but drew primarily upon Brooke's.[6]

In a recent study, Barry Jones broadens the discussion of the literary precursors of *Romeo and Juliet* by taking into account the psychological and cultural basis of literary adaptation. In demonstrating how, progressively, in the Italian versions of the tale the narrative elements combine to form a plot that reflects the social, economic and political realities of the Renaissance city-state,[7] Jones distinguishes between conscious, direct borrowing on the part of authors such as Shakespeare, Brooke, and Boaistuau, and the unconscious borrowings of Da Porto and Bandello, predominantly from the fourth and seventh days of the *Decameron*, that appear to have taken place on the basis of what Jones refers to as "structural and ideological resonances".[8] Thus in attempting to explain Da Porto's change in setting from the Siena of Masuccio's novella to Verona, Jones cites *Decameron* V,8, in which Nastagio's friends and relatives advise him to flee Ravenna before unrequited love brings about his physical and economic downfall. By a process of metathesis, therefore, Boccaccio's Ravenna becomes Da Porto's Verona; likewise Bandello, no less mindful than his predecessor of the example of *Decameron* V,8, models Romeo's infatuation at the beginning of his version of the tale on Nastagio's similar psychological state.[9]

While there can be no disputing the influence of the *Decameron* on numerous aspects of Da Porto's and Bandello's tale, such modifications as these to the setting and plot are better explained by pursuing other features of the novellas which disclose the simultaneous influence, conscious or otherwise, of Boccaccio's near contemporary, the Florentine poet Dante Alighieri (1265–1321), the author of *La Divina Commedia* [*The Divine Comedy*] and, more pertinently here, of *La Vita nuova* [*The New Life*]. Names and places in the tales of Da Porto and Bandello are, on occasion, signs whose collective significance is not so much historical as literary; and it is to Dante that certain signs point.

Given the specificity of time and place established by Da Porto in his introduction—he and his archer are heading towards Udine at the time of the war of the League of Cambrai—it is not surprising that attempts should have been made to identify this archer/narrator with a member of a prominent Veronese family.[10] But this is to miss the point. Dante tells us in the ninth chapter of the *Vita nuova* how he had cause to leave Florence and travel towards the district where the lady who had acted as a screen for Beatrice was living. During the journey Love appears to Dante who is heartsick because he is travelling away from Beatrice: "E però lo dolcissimo segnore, lo quale mi segnoreggiava per la vertù de la gentilissima donna, ne la mia imaginazione apparve come peregrino leggeramente vestito e di vili drappi."[11] [Therefore his very sweet lordship, who ruled over me through the power of that most gracious lady, took the shape in my mind of a pilgrim scantily and poorly dressed].[12] Da Porto's Peregrino, an expert archer, is clearly Dante's "segnore", the definitive archer by association with Cupid. Like Dante, Da Porto declares himself "forse de Amore sospinto" [impelled perhaps by Love] in a mission more amorous than military. In the light of these correspondences, Da Porto's sustained use of a boat metaphor in his dedication to Lucina Savorgnana (he wishes her to be harbour to "[del]la picciola barchetta del mio ingegno"[my mind's small craft] appears rather more as an appropriation of Dante's imagery at the beginning of the *Purgatorio* ("la navicella del mio ingegno" [*Purg.* 1.2: the little bark of my poetic powers]) and in the *Paradiso* ("O voi che siete in piccioletta barca..." [*Par.* 2.1: Oh you that follow in such a light craft]) than as a sexual metaphor deriving from Masuccio Salernitano and Ovid, as has been argued recently.[13]

If, on the one hand, Bandello seemingly rejects Da Porto's Amore/Peregrino assimilation by identifying his own narrator as "il capitano Alessandro Peregrino",[14] on the other hand certain modifications which he brings to Da Porto's plot are clearly inspired as well by the *Vita nuova.* A concerned friend accompanies Dante to a gathering of beautiful women with the intention of distracting him from his unresponsive love; it is here that the poet beholds Beatrice:

> e temendo non altri si fosse accorto del mio tremare, levai li occhi, e mirando le donne, vidi tra loro la gentilissima Beatrice. Allora fuoro sì distrutti li miei spiriti per la forza che Amore prese veggendosi in tanta propinquitade a la gentilissima donna, che non ne rimasero in vita più che li spiriti del viso... (*Vita nuova*, XIV. 4–5) [... and, fearing that people might have become aware of my trembling, I raised my eyes and, looking at the ladies, I saw among them the most gracious Beatrice. Then my spirits were so disrupted by the strength Love acquired when he saw himself this close to the most gracious lady, that none survived except the spirits of sight...].[15]

Bandello likewise has a friend admonish Romeo, infatuated with an unnamed and indifferent woman, urging him to seek a cure for his suffering by attending the city's many masked gatherings. Thus he attends the festivities in the Cappelletti household:

> Quivi era divenuto Romeo consideratore de le bellezze de le donne che erano su la festa, e questa e quella più e meno secondo l'appetito commendava [...] quando gli venne veduta una fuor di misura bellissima garzona che egli non conosceva. Questa infinitamente gli piacque e giudicò che la più bella ed aggraziata giovane non aveva veduta già mai [Romeo set himself up there as judge of the beauty of the women present at the party, and praised in varying degrees this woman and that according to the desire they aroused in him (...) when an indescribably lovely maiden whom he did not know caught his attention. The sight of her gave him immeasurable pleasure and he deemed her to be the most beautiful and charming young woman he had ever seen].[16]

The subsequent correlation between eyes and love is no less attributable to the analogous episode in the *Vita nuova*. Shakespeare will, of course, individualise further Romeo's concerned friend and unresponsive love by giving both a name: Benvolio and Rosaline. Through the mediation of Da Porto and Bandello, Shakespeare's drama is thus indebted to Dante.

Why should Da Porto have chosen to set his tale in Verona during the *signoria* of Bartolomeo della Scala (1301–1304)? Apart from their familiarity with the city—Da Porto was born in Vicenza and Bandello, although born in Lombardy, spent seven years in Verona in the service of Cesare Fregoso—any encomiastic motivation appears unlikely, given that the Della Scala presence in Verona came to an end in 1387. Nor is the projection backwards a strategy to enable criticism of contemporary society, of the kind practised by Machiavelli in his comedy *La mandragola* [The Mandrake Root] (circa 1518). A plausible explanation is to be found in *Paradiso* 17.71–72 where Cacciaguida predicts Dante's banishment. Slandered and exiled, the poet's first refuge will be "la cortesia del gran Lombardo/che 'n su la scala porta il santo uccello;"[17] [the mighty Lombard's courtesy,/ Who on the ladder bears the sacred bird;[18]] Indeed, it appears that Dante first visited Verona in 1304, the year of Bartolomeo della Scala's death, when he also met Francesco, Bartolomeo's younger brother, known as Cangrande, who, Cacciaguida predicts, will bring about great changes in the world. It is, of course, to Cangrande that Dante dedicates the *Paradiso*. Dante celebrates Cangrande della Scala, while Da Porto and his two successors celebrate Cangrande's older brother, the "gran lombardo". Dante looked to Cangrande for peace and unity; the three *novellieri* represent Bartolomeo, described by Da Porto as "signore cortese e umanissimo", [a lord both liberal and kind] as determined to restore civic harmony in Verona by ending the feud between the Montecchi and Cappelletti: between the same two strife-torn families, that is, mentioned in *Purgatorio* 6. 106-107, in the context of Sordello's bitter tirade against the current political state of Italy, described as a ship without a pilot, a brothel, a vicious beast with an empty saddle. It is in this same canto that we are reminded that Sordello and Virgil share the same city of origin: Mantua. And it is to Mantua that the exiled Romeo flees after killing Tebaldo. Verona, as it is represented in these three novellas, appears as a synecdoche for the broader political situation against which Dante rails so vehemently in the *Purgatorio*.

The presence in the novellas of Bartolomeo della Scala and the precise topographical and temporal references, no less than the association of the lovers with two historical families, help to explain the common confusion between historical fact and fiction where the Romeo and Juliet tale is concerned. Indeed, so enduring has been the misconception that the vicissitudes of Romeo and Juliet had their basis in reality, that tourists to Verona today are still able to visit what are purported to be Juliet's balcony and the lovers' tomb.

As Daria Perocco has recently pointed out in the Introduction to her edition of Bandello's tale,[19] belief in the historicity of the Romeo and Giulietta tale persisted until well into the nineteenth century. It is not difficult to see why this should have been so. Where in his tale Masuccio Salernitano limits himself simply to identifying the geographic settings as Siena and Alexandria (in Egypt) and the temporal setting as "non è già gran tempo" [not long ago], Da Porto, imitated subsequently by Bandello and Boaistuau, refers to specific landmarks and customs of Verona during the *signoria* of Bartolomeo della Scala, who, in the novellas of Da Porto, Bandello and Boaistuau, appears in the role of a 'real' city lord adjudicating the feud between fictitious members of two 'real' families, the Montecchi and Cappelletti, within a specific temporal time frame.

There is specificity of place as well in the introduction of the tales by Da Porto and Bandello. At the beginning of his novella Da Porto claims to have heard the story from his Veronese archer as both rode from Gradisca towards Udine; Bandello, in turn, claims to have committed the tale to paper after hearing it narrated at the spa at Caldiero. Only the Frenchman Boaistuau, characteristically reticent about acknowledging his sources, fictional or real, dispenses with this narrative strategy, assuming himself the role of narrator and, occasionally, of commentator. Further adding to the apparent historicity of the tale is the fact that, in accordance with narrative convention, all three authors insist on the veracity of what they are narrating.

Verona is a very real, tangible presence in the novellas, in particular those by Bandello and Boaistuau, both of which begin with a detailed description of the city's most salient topographic features. In both instances, the seemingly aerial perspective of this encomium suggests that its inspiration may have been visual rather than mnemonic. It is as though Bandello—imitated closely by Boaistuau—were looking at an etching and describing what he saw: the Adige, spanned by four bridges, which, he tells us, both divides the city in half and enriches it by allowing trade with Germany; the fertile mountains and valleys surrounding the city; Verona's many fountains and other monuments too numerous to mention (Figure 1).

Figure 1: Verona, 1540

1. The river Adige
2. Castello di San Martino (Castelvecchio)
3. Castello di San Pietro
4. Castello di San Felice
5. The Citadel (cittadella)
6. Communal walls (12th and 13th centuries)
7. Walls of Cangrande della Scala
8. Porta Calzaro
9. Borgo di San Zeno
10. Porta Nuova, opened in the 16th century

Inside the city, much of the narrative action takes place in the monastery of San Francesco, located within the citadel (Figure 2). Indeed, the several references by all three authors both to this "cittadella" and to the Castelvecchio, originally known as the Castello di San Martino in Aquario after a church built on the same site,[20] are evidence that historical accuracy was not of primary concern to them, given that the Castelvecchio was completed on the orders of Cangrande II della Scala some fifty-odd years after the narrative action is meant to have taken place, and the *cittadella* almost 100 years later. Bandello adds to the anachronisms by specifying that the friar carrying Giulietta's letter to Romeo was confined for quarantine reasons to the Franciscan convent in Mantua due to an outbreak of plague; and this despite the fact that plague did not reach northern Italy until 1347. Nor is this sense of place limited to Verona but extends beyond the city's walls as well: upon being banished, Romeo flees to Mantua; Giulietta's father sends her to Villafranca preparatory to her marriage with the Count of Lodrone; Da Porto's disclosure that frate Lorenzo is from Reggio—presumably

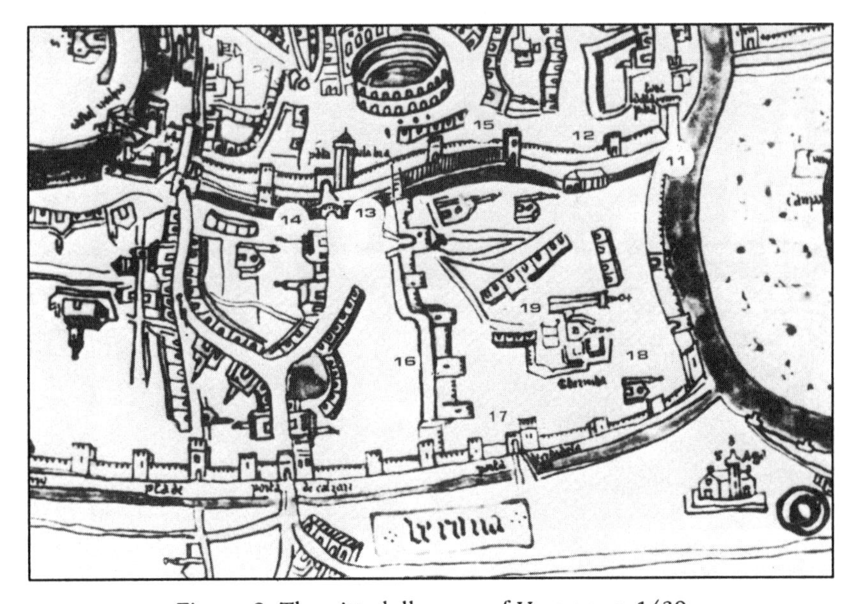


Figure 2: The cittadella area of Verona, c. 1439

11. Torre della Paglia
12. Porta Rofioli
13. Rochetta della Brà
14. Double wall and line of the Adigetto
15. North wall
16. Visconti-Venetian wall
17. Porta di Sant'Antonio, or della Cittadella
18. Sant'Antonio a Corso
19. Santa Trinità

Reggio Emilia rather than Reggio Calabria—is retained by his two successors; and Bandello specifies that the avaricious apothecary responsible for selling poison to Romeo is from Spoleto.

It would be misleading to see in Bandello's overt rejection of Boccaccio as a linguistic model[21] and in all three authors' abandonment of the *cornice* [frame] the desire to emancipate themselves from the narrative tradition that began with the *Decameron*. One of the most striking features of the introduction to Luigi da Porto's novella is, in fact, its affinity with *Decameron* 6,1, the metanarrative tale of madonna Oretta. After dedicating the tale to a distant relative, the noblewoman Lucina Savorgnana, Da Porto tells of the offer made to him by his comrade, Peregrino, to recount a story as they rode through countryside ravaged by warfare; besides serving as a warning to Da Porto of the dangers of love, Peregrino suggests that the narration may serve as a distraction: "... quand'a voi piacesse, potre'io una novella nella mia città avenuta, che la strada men solitaria e men rincrescevole ci faria, raccontarvi..."[22] [... I could tell you, if it should please you, a story that happened in my city, which would make our road appear less lonely and tedious.] The similarities between the two novellas are immediately apparent. Boccaccio gives his voice to his narratee Filomena who, in turn, creates a new story-teller, the *cavaliere*; Da Porto simplifies the pattern somewhat, giving his voice to but one narratee, his companion-in-arms Peregrino. Yet there is a fundamental difference in the strategy employed by Boccaccio and Da Porto: where Boccaccio's readers are privy only to the manner of telling—the content of the *cavaliere*'s tale is not so much as hinted at—what ensues in Da Porto's case is the tale itself rather than the manner of its delivery. Whereas Boccaccio's *cavaliere* is a poor story-teller, confusing names and endlessly repeating himself, Da Porto's is a man of multiple talents, foremost amongst which is his expertise as a story-teller:

> Questi, oltra ch'animoso ed esperto soldato fusse, leggiadro e, forse più di quello ch'agli anni suoi si saria convenuto, innamorato sempre si ritrovava: il che al suo valore doppio valore aggiungneva; onde le più belle novelle e con miglior ordine e grazia si dilettava di raccontare, e massimamente quelle che d'amore parlavano, ch'alcun altro ch'io udissi giamai" [Besides being a brave and expert soldier, Peregrino was handsome and always in love, perhaps more so than became his years. This greatly enhanced his worth, since he delighted in telling the finest stories,

particularly those dealing with love. This he did with more skill and grace than anyone else I have ever heard].[23]

Da Porto's desire to emulate Boccaccio—even to outdo him by having his own narrator excel—is evident. At the same time Da Porto and Bandello, imitated subsequently by Boaistuau, with their introduction of Bartolomeo della Scala and their various embedded Dantesque references, wish to elevate the love of Romeo and Juliet to the ranks of Dante's love for Beatrice.

## Bibliography

The translations in this volume are based on the following Italian and French texts, chosen for their scholarly introductions and philological apparatus. In the case of Da Porto's novella, it is the longer, original version of the tale which has been translated; both versions, however, are included in the volume below, edited by Marziano Guglielminetti.

Salernitano, Masuccio. "Mariotto e Ganozza." *Novelle italiane: Il Quattrocento.* A cura di Gioachino Chiarini. Vol.2. Milano: Garzanti, 1982.

Da Porto, Luigi. "Istoria novellamente ritrovata di due nobili amanti con la loro pietosa morte, intervenuta già nella città di Verona nel tempo del signor Bartolomeo dalla Scala." *Novellieri del Cinquecento.* A cura di Marziano Guglielminetti. Vol.I. Milano-Napoli: Ricciardi, 1972.

Bandello, Matteo. "La sfortunata morte di dui infelicissimi amanti che l'uno di veleno e l'altro di dolore morirono, con vari accidenti." *Novelle di Matteo Bandello.* A cura di Guiseppe Guido Ferrero. Torino: UTET, 1978.

Boaistuau, Pierre. "Histoire troisiesme, De deux amans, dont l'un mourut de venin, l'autre de tristesse." *Histoires Tragiques.* Edition critique publiée par Richard A. Carr. STFM. Paris: Librairie Honoré Champion, 1977.

## Works of Criticism

Given the considerable volume of criticism available on the above authors in Italian, English and French, attention is drawn to the critical works cited in the footnotes to the present Introduction.

Angelo Romano's two-volume anthology, containing most of the Italian versions of the Romeo and Juliet tale together with other related works, is of use to readers of Italian. The bibliographic details for this anthology are as follows:

*Le storie di Giulietta e Romeo.* A cura di Angelo Romano. 2 vols. Roma: Salerno Editrice, 1993.

## Notes

1. The League of Cambrai was an alliance of Pope Julius II, the Holy Roman Emperor Maximilian I, King Louis XII of France, and King Ferdinand of Aragon against the Republic of Venice. In the war which followed, Venice was defeated and the soldiers of the League occupied its territories.
2. See Olin H. Moore, *The Legend of Romeo and Juliet* (Columbus: Ohio State UP, 1950) 38–39. In chapter 4 of this study, Moore summarises the novella "Istorietta amorosa fra Leonora de' Bardi e Ippolito Bondelmonti", highlighting both its affinities with the Romeo and Juliet tale and the discrepancies between the two: Ippolito (rather than Leonora) is the protagonist; there is no sleeping potion; a complicitous abbess (rather than a friar) enables the lovers' rendezvous. In his Introduction to the two-volume anthology *Le storie di Giulietta e Romeo* (Rome: Salerno Editrice, 1993) Angelo Romano attributes the tale "Istorietta amorosa fra Leonora de' Bardi e Ippolito Bondelmonti" to Leon Battista Alberti, thus following in the footsteps of such scholars as Anicio Bonucci and Cecil Grayson. The attribution to Alberti has, however, been questioned, most notably by Judy Rawson in her "The *novella* of *Ippolito e Leonora* and its Attribution to Alberti: A Computer Analysis of Style and Language," *The Languages of Literature in Renaissance Italy*, ed. Peter Hainsworth *et al.* (Oxford: Clarendon Press, 1988) 19–43.

   For further discussion of Shakespeare's sources for *Romeo and Juliet*, see *The Narrative and Dramatic Sources of Shakespeare*, ed. Geoffrey Bullough, vol. 1 (London: Routledge and Kegan Paul; New York: Columbia UP, 1957; 2nd ed. 1961).

3. See Moore 103–10 and Romano 34–35 for discussions of Groto's sources and possible influence on Shakespeare.
4. Lope de Vega's drama has recently been translated into English; see Lope de Vega, *Castelvins and Monteses*, trans. Cynthia Rodriguez-Badendyck (Ottawa: Dovehouse Editions, 1998). For a discussion of Lope de Vega's tragicomedy, see Moore 123–26.
5. Brooke's poem, first published in London in 1562, is reprinted in Bullough (see footnote 2, above), 284–363.
6. See Moore 95.
7. Barry Jones, "*Romeo and Juliet*: the genesis of a classic," *Italian Storytellers: Essays on Italian Narrative Literature*, ed. Eric Haywood and Cormac Ó Cuilleanáin (Dublin: Irish Academic Press, 1989) 152.
8. Jones 151.
9. Jones 171–72.
10. Matteo Bandello, *Giulietta e Romeo*, ed. Daria Perocco (Venice: Marsilio, 1993) 96, note f.
11. Dante Alighieri, *Vita nuova*, in *Opere minori di Dante Alighieri*, ed. Giorgio Bárberi Squarotti, Sergio Cecchin, Angelo Jacomuzzi, Maria Gabriella Stassi (Turin: UTET, 1983) 1X. 3–4. All subsequent quotations from the *Vita nuova* will be taken from this edition.
12. Mark Musa, *Dante's Vita nuova* (Bloomington and London: Indiana UP, 1973) 14. The common noun *peregrino* (or *pellegrino*) means "wayfarer" or "pilgrim" in English; Da Porto adopts Dante's term and converts it into a proper noun. (All subsequent quotations in English will be taken from Musa's translation of the *Vita nuova*.)
13. See Cecil H. Clough, "Love and War in the Veneto: Luigi da Porto and the True Story of *Giulietta e Romeo*," *War, Culture and Society in Renaissance Venice*, ed. David S. Chambers, Cecil H. Clough and Michael E. Mallett (London and Rio Grande: The Hambledon Press, 1993) 99–127; see in particular 123.
14. As Alessandro Bentivoglio was the husband of Ippolita Sforza, the patron who encouraged Bandello to write his novellas, it is possible that the author may have wished to honour Bentivoglio by naming his narrator as he did.
15. Musa 24.
16. Matteo Bandello, "La sfortunata morte di dui infelicissimi amanti che l'uno di veleno e l'altro di dolore morirono, con vari accidenti," *Novelle di Matteo Bandello*, ed. Giuseppe Guido Ferrero (Turin: UTET, 1978) 443.
17. Dante Alighieri, *Paradiso*, vol.3 of *La Divina Commedia*, ed. Natalino Sapegno (Florence: "La Nuova Italia", 1966) 218.

18. Dorothy L. Sayers and Barbara Reynolds, trans., *The Comedy of Dante Alighieri the Florentine. Cantica III. Paradise.* (Harmondsworth: Penguin Books, 1969) 208.
19. Perocco 35, note 20 (see n. 10 above).
20. For information both on the Citadel and the Castelvecchio in Verona, see John E. Law, "The Cittadella of Verona," *War, Culture and Society in Renaissance Venice*, ed. David S. Chambers, Cecil H. Clough and Michael Mallett (London and Rio Grande: The Hambledon Press, 1993) 9–27.
21. Matteo Bandello, "Il Bandello: Ai candidi ed umani lettori," *Tutte le opere*, ed. Francesco Flora (Milan: Mondadori, 1966) 4.
22. Luigi da Porto, "Istoria novellamente ritrovata di due nobili amanti con la loro pietosa morte, intervenuta già nella città di Verona nel tempo del signor Bartolomeo della Scala," *Novellieri del Cinquecento*, ed. Marziano Guglielminetti, vol. 1 (Milan-Naples: Ricciardi, 1972) 246.
23. Da Porto 246. For a discussion of narrative strategy in the *Decameron*, see Sylvie L.F. Richards, "Thrice-Told Tales: Embedded Narratives in the *Decameron* and the *Heptameron*," *Proceedings of the XIIIth Congress of the International Comparative Literature Association, Tokyo 1991*, ed. Will van Peer and Elrud Ibsch (Tokyo: Univ. of Tokyo Press, 293–95), vol. 3, 138–46.

# *Masuccio Salernitano*

## *Novellino* (novella 33)

Mariotto from Siena, in love with Ganozza, flees to Alexandria after becoming a murderer. Ganozza pretends to be dead and, having been taken out of her tomb, goes in search of her lover. Mariotto, having heard of Ganozza's death, seeks his own death by returning to Siena. He is recognised, captured, his head cut off. Not finding Mariotto in Alexandria, Ganozza returns to Siena where she learns her lover has been beheaded. She dies of grief embracing his body.[1]

*To my most illustrious Lord Duke of Amalfi*[2]

### Exordium

The more adverse and ill-fated are love's entanglements, the more one should alert ardent and prudent lovers by writing of love's danger. Since for some considerable time now I have known that you, my most illustrious lord, are not only caught in love's snares but are above all else a most prudent lover, I saw fit to acquaint you fully with the piteous events that befell two unfortunate lovers, so that with your customary prudence and countless virtues you may judge, after giving due consideration to all their actions, which of the two loved more fervently.

### Narrative

The story was told just recently to a gathering of certain fair ladies by a fellow Sienese of yours, of no little authority, how, not long ago in Siena, there was a youth of good family, as upright as he was handsome, one Mariotto Mignanelli who, being passionately in love with a fair young maiden called Ganozza, the daughter of an eminent and highly esteemed citizen, possibly of the Saraceni family, in due course was loved most ardently by her in like measure. The young maid, as wise as she was beautiful, feasted her eyes for some time on love's bright flowers, and no less eager than Mariotto to taste its honey-sweet fruit, sought different ways of achieving this end, but rejected them all as imprudent. She thus resolved to take him secretly as her husband, so that if by some misfortune their enjoyment were forbidden, they would be shielded from all censure. In order to bring this about, they bribed an Augustinian friar by means of whom they secretly contracted this marriage. Emboldened then by such an infallible precaution, they satisfied fully their burning desires, with equal pleasure to both.

After they had happily enjoyed for a time their secret and, to a degree licit love, it happened that fortune, evil and adverse, upset all their present and future desires. This came about one day when Mariotto, in an argument with another honourable citizen, passed from words to deeds, dealing him a fatal blow to the head with a stick, from which he died a few days later. Mariotto went into hiding and, having been sought diligently but in vain by the authorities, was not only condemned to perpetual exile by the city lords and *podestà*,[3] but was also proclaimed an enemy of the city.

Only those who have suffered similar pangs can truly appreciate the extreme grief and bitter tears of the two stricken lovers, secretly wed for so short a time, faced with such a protracted and, as they believed, permanent separation. Their grief was so intense and bitter that both often appeared lifeless as they embraced while taking their final leave of one another. After venting his grief somewhat, and hoping that his return to Siena would be granted following some unforeseeable turn of events, Mariotto resolved with equal determination to leave behind not only Tuscany but Italy, and to go to Alexandria where he had an uncle, Ser Nicolò Mignanelli by name, a well-known public figure and merchant. Amidst copious tears, the enamoured pair took leave of one another after arranging to keep in touch by letter, despite the distance separating them.

Mariotto departed full of sorrow, having confided his private affairs to his brother. Above all else, Mariotto entreated him to send detailed and frequent accounts of all that befell his Ganozza. After giving these orders, he then headed for Alexandria. He arrived there in due course and, once he had found his overjoyed uncle and was lovingly received by him, informed him of all that had happened. This uncle, being a most prudent man, was aggrieved at learning not so much of the murder that had been committed as of the wrong done to such a family. Realising that recrimination would serve no purpose, he counselled Mariotto to set his mind to rest and to think how, in time, he could make amends. The uncle then entrusted some of his business transactions to Mariotto, all the while commiserating with him and making him warmly welcome. Yet not a month went by that Mariotto did not receive news from Ganozza and his brother, which was a wondrous consolation to all concerned for the cruel circumstances and lengthy separation.

This was the state of affairs when Ganozza's father, pressured by many suitors, all of whom Ganozza rejected with convincing arguments, was finally so insistent that his daughter take a husband that any further refusal on Ganozza's part would clearly have been pointless. So keen and unrelenting was her mental anguish that she would willingly have renounced life in favour of death. Moreover, she had given up all hope that her beloved, clandestine husband would return and realised that revealing the truth to her father would have worsened the situation rather than helped it. She thus decided to put an end to her problems in a way which was not only unusual but extreme and fraught with danger, perhaps even unheard-of, and which would imperil her reputation and life.

Assisted by her great courage and having told her father that she would comply with his every wish, Ganozza at once sent for the priest who had thought up the idea in the first place. She took great heed in revealing to him what she intended to do and asked him to favour her with his help. The priest appeared somewhat astonished at her words, as is common with his kind, but Ganozza, using the singular charms of Mammon,[4] changed his reticence and reluctance into intrepid eagerness to execute the plan without heed to danger. Since they had no time to lose, the friar himself, in keeping with one well-versed in such matters, hastened to concoct a certain potion blended from various powders in such a way that, once Ganozza had drunk it, not only would it make her sleep for three days but she would be deemed well and truly dead by everyone. He sent it to the woman, who drank it with great pleasure, after first encharging a messenger to inform Mariotto fully of her intentions and receiving instructions from the friar about what she was to do.

Shortly thereafter she was overcome by such a profound stupor that she fell to the ground as though dead. Her aged father came running with many other members of the household at the noise of the outcry made by Ganozza's chambermaids. Having found his dearly beloved only daughter already dead, overwhelmed by grief without precedent he immediately sent for doctors, who tried every means at their disposal to bring her back to life, but to no avail. They all concluded that a fatal stroke was responsible for her death. A constant vigil was kept over her in the house all that day and the following night, but as she gave no signs of life, she was buried the next day with great pomp in a magnificent tomb in the church of St Augustine, to the boundless grief of her broken-hearted father and the weeping and sorrow of relatives, friends, and all the citizens of Siena in general.

Around midnight, the venerable friar removed Ganozza from the tomb with the help of a friend and took her to his room according to plan. As the time was already approaching when the draught was to have run its course, they managed at last to bring her back to life with the help of warmth from the fire and other necessary measures.

Ganozza had completely recovered her senses when, a few days later, disguised as a friar, she travelled with the good priest to Porto Pisano where the galleys from Aigues Mortes[5] were to make port en route to Alexandria. Having found this was so, they embarked. And since inclement weather and unforeseen needs on the part of merchants tend to draw sea voyages out more than travellers would want, it so chanced that for various reasons the galleys arrived months behind schedule.

Mariotto's brother, Gargano, in order to carry out the instructions left to him by his brother, had immediately entrusted to traders a number of different letters in which with boundless regret he informed the luckless Mariotto of all the details of Ganozza's sudden death, where and how she had been mourned and buried, and how, shortly after, grief had caused her aged and loving father to pass from this life. Meddlesome misfortune was much more favourable to this news than it had been to the messenger sent by the grieving Ganozza, perhaps because it was to blame for preparing the bitter and bloody end with which they were to meet.

Thus it was that her messenger, while on a caravel sailing to Alexandria with a cargo of wheat, was captured by pirates and killed, with the result that the only news to reach Mariotto was his brother's, which he believed without question. If there is any pity in your heart, oh reader, you can imagine Mariotto's rightful pain and sorrow at this most bitter news. Despite his dear uncle's vain attempts at comfort and dissuasion, Mariotto's grief was so profound that he resolved to put an end to his life. After lengthy and bitter weeping, he finally decided to return to Siena where, if fortune for once favoured him by keeping his return secret, he would remain, disguised, at the foot of the tomb wherein he believed his Ganozza to be buried and there hasten his own death with his copious tears. And if, by mischance, he were to be recognised, he would welcome being executed as a murderer, believing already dead she whom he loved more than himself and by whom he had been loved in equal measure.

Thus resolved, Mariotto waited for the Venetian galleys to leave for the west and, without saying a word to his uncle, he embarked, hastening towards his predestined death with the greatest pleasure. He arrived in Naples after only a short time and from there having journeyed by land to Tuscany as quickly as possible, he entered Siena unrecognised, disguised as a pilgrim. Having sought refuge in an unfrequented inn and without saying a word to anyone, when the time was right he took himself off to the church where his Ganozza was buried. He wept bitterly before her sepulchre and, had he been able, he would willingly have entered the tomb so that in dying he could unite his body for all eternity with that most fair which he had not been permitted to enjoy while living. All his thoughts were set on carrying this out.

Never ceasing his accustomed lamentations and constant tears, he hid himself inside the church one evening around sunset after having discreetly obtained some tools. With nightfall he at last managed to prop the tomb lid open and was about to go in when it chanced that the sacristan, on his way to ring the bells for matins, heard a certain noise. When he went to investigate, he found Mariotto thus occupied and, believing him a thief set on robbing the dead, yelled loudly: "Thief! Thief!" All the friars came running, seized Mariotto, and opened the doors. A crowd of people poured in and found the wretched lover who, although still dressed in lowly rags, was immediately recognised as Mariotto Mignanelli and detained there. Before daybreak, all Siena was full of the news.

When the city lords heard of it, they ordered the *podestà* to seize Mariotto and do with him what the law and their constitution demanded. Thus captured and bound, Mariotto was brought to the *podestà*'s palace where he was hoisted up by a rope and let drop,[6] but little torture was required to make him confess precisely why he had returned so rashly. Even though everyone felt great pity for him and the women present, each of whom would have redeemed him with her own blood, wept bitterly, looking upon him as a uniquely perfect lover, nevertheless he was condemned by the authorities to lose his head early the following morning. And so the sentence was carried out at the appointed time, his friends and relatives having been powerless to prevent it.

Wretched Ganozza who, after several months and many trials arrived in Alexandria escorted by the aforementioned friar, found her way to Ser Nicolò's house. Once she had made herself known and told him who she was and why she had come, and recounted all her other past troubles to him, he was filled at once with amazement and sorrow. After he had received her with honour, he had her clothed in women's attire and dismissed the friar. He then told the unfortunate young woman how her Mariotto, in despair because of the news of her death, had departed without warning, and how he had wept for Mariotto believing him dead, given that he had gone for no other reason than to die.

Let those who are able to and must, consider after due thought whether it was reasonable for Ganozza's present great sorrow to surpass all other that both she and her lover had previously experienced, since to my mind words could not describe it. After Ganozza had thus returned to her senses and sought counsel of her new father, she and Ser Nicolò, having deliberated at length, weeping burning tears, decided to return with all haste to Siena where, whether they found Mariotto dead or alive, they could at least restore the woman's reputation by whatever means available to them in such extreme circumstances.

Once Ser Nicolò had settled his affairs as best he could and the woman had again donned male attire, they sailed with a favourable wind, reaching the shores of Tuscany after a swift and uneventful passage. They disembarked at Piombino and from there journeyed secretly to an estate of Ser Nicolò's near Siena. Upon asking for news, they learned that their Mariotto had been beheaded three days earlier.

While not doubting the truth of this most cruel news, they nevertheless sought to confirm it. Just how numbed and filled with grief they both were, the tragic nature of the ensuing events will demonstrate. Ganozza's weeping and wailing were impassioned enough to move a heart of stone to pity. Although she was constantly comforted by Ser Nicolò, following much wise and loving advice from him they resolved, after so great a loss, simply to look to the reputation of such an eminent family and arrange for the poor young woman to be admitted secretly to a most holy convent, where she might spend the rest of her days bitterly weeping both her own misfortunes and wretchedness and the death of her dear lover. This was carried out with the utmost caution. Once there Ganozza, without disclosing anything about herself except to the abbess, consumed by inner grief and bitter tears, with little food and no sleep, ever calling her Mariotto, forthwith ended her wretched days.

## Masuccio

All these adverse events will have moved feeling women much more than virile men to double pity. Moreover, women will judge Ganozza's love to be unparalleled, more intense even than her lover's. Yet should there by chance be present at such a discussion someone who loves wisely, he will offer convincing arguments that the love of wretched Mariotto was incomparably greater and more passionate. The reason for this is that Ganozza, even if she resorted to means remarkable for a woman in seeking out her lover, was motivated by the belief that she would find him alive, and would then share a long and pleasurable life with him. But Ganozza's hapless lover, hearing of her death, wanted to return with all haste for no other reason than to lose his own life, which he did.

# *Luigi da Porto*

"Istoria novellamente ritrovata di due nobili amanti con la loro pietosa morte, intervenuta già nella città di Verona nel tempo del signor Bartolomeo dalla Scala."

*A tale*
*recently come to light, about two noble lovers and their pitiful death, which took place in the city of Verona during the time of Lord Bartolomeo della Scala*[7]

*To the most beautiful and fair Madonna Lucina Savorgnana*

After I mentioned to you in person some time ago that I wished to write down a moving story which I have heard several times and which took place in Verona, I felt it only right to relate it to you in these few pages. This I do in order to keep my promise to you, but also because it befits a lovelorn wretch like myself to speak of such lovers' woes as abound in this tale. Mindful of your virtue, I am sending it to you so that on reading it you may more clearly see—even though I know that it is your great wisdom which sets you apart from other beautiful women—to what risks, to what reckless passes, to what grievous deaths wretched and unfortunate lovers may often be driven by Love.

No less mindful of your beauty also, I am sending my tale willingly to you so that with you my foolish flights of fancy may cease, since I have resolved that this is to be my last literary effort, for I have already had my fill of being the subject of idle talk. As you are harbour to virtue, beauty, and grace, I have further resolved that you will be harbour to my mind's small craft which, weighed down with ignorance and driven on by Love, has long ploughed poetry's shallower waters. Fully cognisant of her grave error and relinquishing rudder, oars, and sail to others who navigate this sea guided by greater learning and a better star, on reaching you may she thus find safe anchorage disarmed on your shores. Accept, therefore, my tale, Madonna, in the form befitting it, and read it with pleasure both for its subject matter, which is not only most beautiful but also, I believe, very moving, as well as for the close family ties and sweet friendship existing between your own person and he who writes the tale down. It is with all due reverence that he ever commends himself to you.

As you yourself witnessed, in the early years of my youth I took up arms when heaven still had not turned the full force of its wrath against me. In the service of many great and valiant men I practised this profession for several years in Friuli, your delightful birthplace, where my service compelled me to go hither and thither, according to circumstances both professional and private. I was accustomed to taking one of my archers with me on my travels, a most agreeable man named Peregrino, about fifty years old and an expert archer who, in common with most people from Verona, his birthplace, was given to talking a great deal. Besides being a brave and expert soldier, Peregrino was handsome and always in love, perhaps more so than became his years. This greatly enhanced his worth, since he delighted in telling the finest stories, particularly those dealing with love. This he did with more skill and grace than anyone else I have ever heard.

It was for this reason that, as I set out with him and two other men of mine from Gradisca where I had been camped, impelled perhaps by Love, heading towards Udine along a very lonely road ravaged and burnt by the recent war[8] and weighed down by my thoughts, when I became separated from the others Peregrino drew close to me and, as one who guessed my thoughts, spoke to me thus: "Do you wish always to live a life of unhappiness because a beautiful, cruel woman cares little for you while pretending otherwise? And even though by speaking to you thus I am also indirectly rebuking myself, since it is easier to give advice than to follow it, still I shall tell you, my lord, that not only is it unseemly for someone of your profession to dwell at length in Love's prison, but it is also dangerous to follow Love, so unhappy almost without exception is the outcome to which he leads us. As proof of this I could tell you, if it should please you, a story that happened in my city, which would make our road appear less lonely and tedious. In this tale you will hear how two noble lovers were led to a wretched and pitiful death." After I had indicated my eagerness to hear him, he began as follows.

During the time that Bartolomeo della Scala, a lord both liberal and kind, held the reins of power in my beautiful city, there lived in Verona two very noble families, the Capelletti and the Montecchi who, according to what my father claimed to have heard, were enemies, either because of their conflicting political allegiances or because of some specific cause for hatred. It is thought that Messer Nicolò and Messer Giovanni, at present living in Udine, are descendants of the Montecchi, but are now called the Monticoli from Verona, having left this city following a grievous event, although little else of their ancestors did they take away with them apart from their courtly gentility. And although I read in some old chronicles of these two families having supported the same political faction, still I shall tell the tale to you just as I heard it, without changing it in any way.

Thus as I said, there lived in Verona under the aforementioned lord these two very noble families, both equally endowed by heaven, nature, and fortune with wealth and men of valour. For whatever reason a most bitter feud reigned between them, as frequently happens with great families. Many men on both sides had already been killed because of this feud, with the result that weariness, as often happens in such cases, no less than the threats of the city's lord, whose displeasure at seeing them enemies was considerable, had prompted them to refrain from further strife. Without any public reconciliation having taken place, in time they were reconciled to the extent that many of their men were talking to each other.

With peace thus restored between them, it happened one Carnival that, in the house of Messer Antonio, the merry and spirited head of the Capelletti family, many festivities were held both day and night, attended by almost the entire city. As is the habit of lovers who, whenever possible, follow their lady love with heart and body wherever she goes, one night a youth from the Montecchi family took himself to one of these festivities in pursuit of his lady. This youth was very handsome, of imposing stature, graceful, and well-mannered. It is for this reason that, once he had removed his mask as everyone else was doing and, dressed as a nymph as he was, all eyes turned to look at him, not only for his beauty, which exceeded that of all the women present, but also out of amazement that he should have come to that house, especially at night. More than anyone else, the sight of him impressed the only daughter of the said Messer Antonio,[9] a maiden of unmatched beauty, as spirited as she was fair, who, having beheld the youth, was so struck by his good looks that from the moment their eyes first met it seemed to her that she was no longer mistress of herself.

This youth remained apart from the others at the party, all alone and unsure of himself, and rarely did he join in the dancing or conversation, as one who, drawn to that house by Love, now felt very uneasy there. This grieved the maiden greatly, because she had heard that he was most charming and fun-loving. Once midnight had passed and the festivities were drawing to a close, there began the dance of the torch or hat,[10] however we may wish to call it, still used to bring festivities to an end. In this dance, in which men and women form a circle and change partners at will, no woman chose the young man who, by chance, found himself next to the already enamoured maiden. On her other side was a young nobleman, known as Marcuccio the Cross-Eyed, whose hands were habitually very cold, in July no less than in January. Thus when Romeo Montecchi—for this was the young man's name—arrived on the woman's left and, as is done in this dance, took her fair hand in his, the maid said to him almost immediately, perhaps eager to hear him speak: "Praised be your arrival here at my side, Messer Romeo."

The youth, who had already noticed her glances, replied in amazement at her words: "What do you mean, praised be my arrival?" And she answered: "Yes, praised be your arrival at my side, because you at least will keep my left hand warm while Marcuccio freezes my right one." Romeo, somewhat emboldened, continued: "If I warm your hand with mine, you set my heart on fire with your beautiful eyes." After a fleeting smile the woman spoke further to him, taking care not to be seen with him or heard speaking to him: "I swear to you Romeo, on my faith, that no woman present appears as beautiful to my eyes as you do." To which the youth replied, already aflame: "Whatever I may be, should it not displease your beauty, I shall be its faithful servant." Having left the festivities shortly afterwards, Romeo returned to his own home where, after giving thought to the cruelty of his former love, who granted him scant reward for his considerable suffering, he resolved to devote himself wholly to her, should she so wish, even though she belonged to the enemy faction.

On the other hand the maiden, thinking of little else but him, after much sighing deemed that she would ever be happy if she could have him as her husband. But because of the feud between the two families, she greatly feared that there was little hope of achieving such a happy outcome. Thus living ever prey to two opposing thoughts, she repeated to herself: "Oh fool that I am, for what vain hope am I allowing myself to be led into this strange labyrinth? I shall be alone there, unable to find my way out at will, since Romeo Montecchi loves me not. As there is a feud between his family and mine, he cannot be seeking other than my dishonour. And even supposing he wanted me as his wife, my father would never consent to give me to him." Changing then her way of thinking, she said: "Who knows, in order to consolidate the peace between these two families that are already sick and tired of feuding, perhaps it could still come about that I have him the way I want!" And dwelling on this thought, she began granting him now and then the courtesy of her gaze.

With both lovers thus equally aflame and bearing the dear name and image of the other engraved in their hearts, they began to look lovingly upon one another, sometimes in church or at some window, with the result that their well-being depended upon seeing one another. He above all was so enflamed by her charming ways that he passed almost the entire night alone in front of her house, at great risk to his life. Sometimes he climbed up on the balcony outside her bedroom window where, without her or anyone else knowing, he would sit and listen to her beautiful voice; at other times he would lie in the street.

As Love would have it, one night when the moon was shining more brightly than usual it happened that, while Romeo was climbing onto this balcony, the maiden came to open the window, either by chance or because she had heard him the other evenings; and leaning out, she saw him. Believing that not she but someone else had opened the balcony window, Romeo made as if to flee into the shadow of some wall. Having realised who it was and calling him by name, she said to him: "What are you doing here all alone at this hour?" And he, having by this time recognised her, replied: "That which Love wills." "And if you were to be caught," said the woman, "could you not easily lose your life?" "My lady," replied Romeo, "it is true that I could easily lose my life, and I surely shall one night, if you do not help me. But since I am as near to death everywhere else as I am here, I am striving to die as close as I can to your person, with which I yearn to live forever, should you and heaven so please."

To this the maiden replied: "I shall never be to blame if you do not live honestly with me. If only it no longer depended on you or on the enmity I see dividing your family and mine!" The youth replied: "You can be assured that it is not possible to long for something more than I constantly long for you! Thus if it should please you to be mine as I wish to be yours, I shall do so willingly, nor shall I fear that another will ever take you from me." After saying this and arranging to speak to each other at greater leisure some other night, they both departed.

Having subsequently returned various times to talk to her, one evening when it was snowing heavily the youth met her again at the longed for place and said to her: "Ah, why do you make me suffer like this? Do you feel no pity for me, that every night in weather like this I wait for you here in this street?" To this the woman replied: "Certainly I pity you, but what do you want me to do, if not beg you to go away?" The young man replied: "I would ask that you let me come into your room, where we would be able to converse in greater comfort." The fair maiden then replied, almost in anger: "Romeo, I love you as much as one can rightfully love anyone, and I grant you more than befits my virtue. This I do won over by love and your high worth. But if you think that by courting me for a long time or by any other means to enjoy my love in any way other than as my beloved, then banish this thought, because it will avail you nothing. And to spare you the danger in which I see you place your life every night by coming to these parts, I declare that, if you should see fit to accept me as your wife, I am willing to give myself wholly to you and to accompany you unhesitatingly wherever it pleases you to go." "This is my sole desire," said the youth, "let it be done now." "Let it be done," replied the woman, "but let it then be repeated in the presence of my confessor, Frate Lorenzo of the Order of St Francis, if you wish me to give myself wholly and happily to you." "Oh," Romeo said to her, "so it is Frate Lorenzo from Reggio who knows your heart's every secret?" "Yes," she replied, "and to satisfy me let him be witness to all we do." And having arranged their affairs carefully, they took leave of one another.

Besides being a member of the Minor Order of observance, this friar was a great philosopher and an expert in natural and supernatural phenomena alike;[11] and such was the friendship between him and Romeo that it would have been difficult at that time to find two closer friends anywhere. Thus as the friar wished to remain in the good graces of his flock whilst indulging at the same time in several of his illicit pleasures, it had been in his best interests to take several of the city's noblemen into his confidence. From amongst these he had singled out Romeo, a youth regarded with fear, as spirited as he was prudent, and to him he revealed his innermost secrets, which to all others he kept hidden by pretending.

Once Romeo had found him, he thus freely explained to the friar how he wished to have the maiden he loved as his wife, and how together they had decided that he alone was to be secret witness to their wedding, thereafter acting on their behalf in persuading her father to accept it. The friar agreed to this, both because he could deny Romeo nothing without bringing serious harm upon himself, and perhaps even more because he thought that through his doing the situation would have a happy outcome, which would place him in excellent standing with the city lord and all others who wished to see these two families reconciled.

As it was Lent, one day the maiden went to the monastery of St Francis, pretending that she wished to have her confession heard. Having gone into one of those confessionals used by these friars, she sent for Frate Lorenzo. Hearing that she was there, the friar, accompanied by Romeo, entered the same confessional from within the convent and, having both locked the door and removed the iron grate that separated them from the maiden, said to her: "It is my practice to see you most willingly, but here and now you are dearer to me than ever, if it is true that you wish my lord Romeo for your husband." To which she replied: "There is nothing I want more than to be legitimately his, and for this reason I have come here before you whom I trust completely, so that you and God may witness what I have come to do, driven by love." Thus in the presence of the friar who agreed to keep everything secret, with the appropriate vow Romeo then wed the beautiful maid.[12] Once they had arranged to meet the following night and had kissed one another just once, they took their leave of the friar who, after replacing the grate in the wall, stayed to hear the confession of other women.

Having become clandestinely husband and wife in the way that you have heard, the two lovers happily enjoyed their love for several nights, biding their time until they could find some way to win over the woman's father, who they knew would be opposed to their desires. Thus was the situation when it happened that Fortune, the enemy of every worldly pleasure, revived the almost forgotten feud between their families by spreading I know not what evil seed so that things were thrown into turmoil. In the main street the Montecchi and Capelletti set upon each other on one occasion, and neither family was prepared to give way to the other. As Romeo fought he took care not to strike any member of his wife's family out of consideration for her. Yet finally, as many of his own family had been wounded and almost all of them chased from the street, Romeo, overcome by fury, fell upon Tebaldo Capelletti who appeared to be the most formidable of his enemies, and sent him to the ground with a mortal blow; and the others, who were already in disarray because of the death of Tebaldo, he sent fleeing.

Romeo had been seen wounding Tebaldo, so the murder could not be covered up. Thus when suit was brought before the city lord, each and every one of the Capelletti accused Romeo alone, so that the court banished him for ever from Verona. Every woman who truly loves can easily imagine by putting herself in the wretched maiden's place how she felt on beholding these events. Her weeping was so constant and overwhelming that no one could console her; and her grief was all the more bitter the less she dared reveal its cause to anyone.

On the other hand, leaving his native city grieved the youth because it meant forsaking her. Refusing to depart without taking tearful leave of her and not being able to go to her house, he turned to the friar, instructing him to send word through one of her father's servants, a good friend of Romeo's, that she was to come, which she did. After they had both gone into the confessional, together they lamented at length their misfortune. Finally she said to him: "What will I do without you? I no longer have the heart to go on living. It would be better that I accompanied you wherever you might go. I shall cut my hair and follow you as your servant; nor could anyone serve you better or more faithfully than I." "May it not please God, dear heart of mine, that, at such time as you were to come with me, I should take you in any form other than as my wife," Romeo said to her. "But since I am certain that things cannot remain like this for long, and that peace between our families will shortly follow, whereupon I could easily beg the lord of the city for pardon again, I want you to remain without my body for a few days because my soul dwells ever with you. And should things not come about as I propose, we will find some other solution to our predicament." With this settled between them, they embraced a thousand times and took their leave of one another weeping all the while, the woman imploring him to remain as close to her as he could and not to go to Rome or Florence as he had said he would.

Romeo, who until then had been hiding in Frate Lorenzo's monastery, left a few days later and almost dead from grief sought refuge in Mantua, having first told the woman's servant that he was to let the friar know immediately of anything he heard said about his lady in the house, and that he was to do faithfully everything the maiden ordered if he wished to receive the rest of the reward that had been promised to him.

Even after Romeo had been gone for many days the maiden was still weeping, which faded her great beauty. Her mother, who loved her dearly, asked her affectionately several times the cause of her weeping, saying: "Oh my daughter, as dear to me as life itself, what is this grief that has been tormenting you for a while now? Why is it that you cannot refrain from weeping for even a short time? If perhaps you yearn for something, confide it to me alone, for I shall gratify you in anything that decency allows me to." Despite this the maiden always gave her feeble excuses for her grief.

Thus one day the mother, thinking that her daughter's grief sprang from a secret desire to be wed which she kept hidden, whether through modesty or fear, said one day to her husband in the belief that she was seeking her daughter's welfare, whereas in fact she was bringing about her death: "Messer Antonio, for many days now I have seen this daughter of ours do nothing but weep, with the result that she no longer appears herself, as you can see. And though I have questioned her repeatedly about the cause of her grief, I can get nothing from her. Neither could I say myself what causes it, unless it is perhaps due to a desire to be wed which, wise as she is, she dares not reveal. Thus before she wastes away any more, I would advise that she be given a husband. Besides, she turned eighteen years of age this past St Euphemia's day[13] and beyond this age women become less rather than more beautiful. Moreover, they are not merchandise that should be kept in the house for any length of time, although I know that our daughter's behaviour has always been above reproach. I am aware that you already provided for her dowry some days ago, so let us see to giving her a fitting husband."

Messer Antonio answered that it would be wise to marry her and commended his daughter highly for preferring to suffer over this desire of hers rather than appeal to him or to her mother; and within a few days he began to negotiate her marriage to a count of the Lodrone family. As he was about to finalise negotiations, the mother said to her daughter, believing that she would cause her great pleasure: "You can cheer up now, my daughter, for within a few days you will be honourably married to a great nobleman and you will no longer have cause to weep. Although you wouldn't tell me what the matter was, through God's grace I understood it and your father and I have taken steps to make you happy."[14]

Hearing these words the beautiful maid could no longer hold back her tears, hence her mother said to her: "Do you think I am telling a lie? In less than eight days you will be the wife of a handsome young nobleman of the Lodrone family." At these words the maiden began weeping even more bitterly, so her mother, cajoling her, said: "Well then, my daughter, will you agree to this?" To which she replied: "No, never, mother, shall I agree to it." To this her mother added: "What then do you want? Tell me, for I am prepared to do anything for you." The maiden then said: "Just to die." Whereupon Madonna Giovanna (for such was the mother's name), being a wise woman understood that her daughter was burning with love; and after answering her I know not what, she left her.

That evening when her husband came she repeated to him what their daughter, weeping, had answered. This displeased him greatly, and he thought it prudent to sound out her thoughts on the matter before the wedding negotiations proceeded any further so as not to bring any shame upon themselves. And having had her brought one day before him, he said to her: "Giulietta," for this was the maiden's name, "I am about to marry you nobly: do you agree to this, daughter?" The maiden finally broke her silence following his words by replying: "No, father, I shall never agree to it." "What? Do you wish to become a nun?" asked her father. And she replied, her words and tears spilling out together: "I don't know, sire." To this her father answered: "I know that this is not what you want. Accept the fact that I intend marrying you to a count of the Lodrone family." The maiden replied, sobbing: "This will never be." Then very irate, Messer Antonio threatened to beat her if she persisted in opposing his will, and if besides this she did not disclose the cause of her grief. And failing to extract anything from her but tears, highly displeased he left her

with Madonna Giovanna; and it was equally impossible for h
fathom her daughter's thoughts.

The maiden had related her mother's words to Pietro, a servant in her father's employ who was aware of her love, and in his presence she had vowed she would drink poison of her own free will rather than take anyone other than Romeo as her husband, even if she were able. According to instructions, Pietro had informed Romeo of all this by means of the friar, and Romeo had written to Giulietta that under no circumstances was she to agree to marry, and even less was she to disclose their love, for within eight to ten days without fail he would find a way to get her out of her father's house.

But both endearments and threats proved ineffectual to Messer Antonio and Madonna Giovanna in eliciting from their daughter the reason why she did not want to marry; nor could they discover the object of her affections in any other way. Madonna Giovanna reiterated to her a number of times: "Come now, my darling daughter, cry no more, for you will be granted the husband of your choice, even if it were one of the Montecchi you wanted, which I am certain you would not;" and as Giulietta gave her no reply apart from sighs and weeping, more suspicious than ever they resolved to finalise as soon as possible the marriage they had negotiated between her and the Count of Lodrone.

On hearing of this, the maiden was overcome with grief and not knowing what to do, she wished for death a thousand times a day. Yet she determined to make her grief known to Frate Lorenzo as someone whom, after Romeo, she most trusted and who, from what she had heard from her lover, knew how to perform many great deeds. Thus one day she said to Madonna Giovanna: "Mother, I don't want you to be surprised if I don't tell you what makes me weep, as I myself do not know. All I can say is that I constantly feel such sadness as makes not only other people's but my own life wretched. I don't know why I feel like this, and even less can I explain it to you or to my father, unless it was caused by some forgotten sin that I committed. Since my last confession was of great benefit to me, I would like, should it so please you, to make another confession so that this coming Pentecost I might ease my sorrow by receiving the sweet medicine of the holy body of our Lord." Madonna Giovanna agreed to this and two days later, having accompanied her to the convent of St Francis, she left her with Frate Lorenzo, having first entreated him to try and learn from her confession the cause of her sorrow.

As soon as the maiden saw that her mother was no longer within earshot, she immediately recounted all her woes to the friar in a sorrowful voice, begging him in the name of the love and close friendship that she knew bound him to Romeo, to help her in her great need. The friar replied: "What can I possibly do in this instance, my daughter, with such enmity existing between your family and your husband's?" The sorrowful maid replied: "I am aware that you know many unusual things and in a thousand ways you can help me, if you want to; but grant me at least this one favour, if no other. I hear that they are making preparations for my wedding in one of my father's palaces, about two miles from this city going towards Mantua. They intend taking me there so as to weaken my resolve not to accept my new husband, and no sooner shall I reach there than he who is supposed to marry me will also arrive. Give me however much poison is necessary to free both me from suffering such as this and Romeo from such dishonour. If you do not, I shall cause even greater harm to myself and grief to him by staining a knife with my blood."

Frate Lorenzo, hearing her determination and thinking to what extent he was still bound to Romeo who would undoubtedly become his enemy if he did not take care of this matter, spoke thus to the maiden: "Look, Giulietta, as you know half this city comes to me for confession and I am well regarded by everyone, so much so that I always intervene whenever a will is drawn up or peace is made. Thus not for all the gold in the world would I wish to be involved in any scandal or for it to be known that I had a hand in this business. Yet because I love both you and Romeo, I am prepared to do what I have never done for anyone else, as long as you promise not to disclose my role in it." To which the maiden replied: "Father, give me the poison without fear, because nobody apart from myself will ever know about it." He answered: "It is not poison that I shall give you, my daughter, because it would be too great a pity[15] if one as young and beautiful as you were to die. But if you have the courage to do what I say, I am sure that I can lead you safely to your Romeo."

"As you know," he continued, "the Capelletti crypt is situated outside this church, in our cemetery. I shall give you a powder which, once you have drunk it, for around forty-eight hours will make you sleep in such a way that no one, not even the greatest doctor, will deem you anything but dead. You will undoubtedly be buried in the said crypt as though you had passed from this life. At the right moment I shall come, take you out and keep you in my cell until I go to the forthcoming meeting of our order, which we hold in Mantua. I shall escort you there to your husband, disguised in our habit. But tell me, won't you be afraid of the body of your cousin Tebaldo, who was buried in there just recently?" The maiden replied, already in good spirits: "Father, if going through Hell meant rejoining Romeo, I would not hesitate to do it." "Well, then," he said, "since you feel like that, I agree to help you. But before we do anything else I think you should personally inform Romeo of everything by letter so that despair does not make him do something drastic if he believes you dead, because I know he loves you greatly. I always have friars going to Mantua where, as you know, Romeo is. Let me have the letter, which I shall send to him by means of a trusted messenger."

Having said this the good friar, without the likes of whom no great undertaking can be successfully concluded, left the maiden in the confessional and hastened to his cell. He returned to her immediately with a tiny phial of powder and said: "Take this powder, and around three or four in the morning—whenever you think best—you are to drink it without fear, dissolved in cold water. It will start to take effect around six, and our plan will surely succeed. But so that it may, do not forget to send me the letter you have to write to Romeo, for it is very important."

After taking the powder, Giulietta returned to her mother light-hearted and said: "My lady, Frate Lorenzo is truly the best confessor in the world. He has comforted me so much that I no longer recall my past unhappiness." Madonna Giovanna replied, herself gladdened by her daughter's cheerfulness: "Willingly, my child, will you on occasion see to consoling him with our charity, because they are poor friars." And speaking thus, they went off home.

After this confession Giulietta was in such good spirits that Messer Antonio and Madonna Giovanna had put aside all thought of her being in love, believing instead that some unusual, inexplicable sorrow had caused her weeping. They would willingly have let her be for the time being, abandoning all talk of giving her a husband, but they had proceeded so far with this matter that they could not withdraw from the negotiations without causing offence. Thus it was arranged that the maiden was to go to her father's aforementioned palace just outside the city, in the company of two of her aunts, since Count Lodrone wished someone from his family to take a look at her as Madonna Giovanna, her mother, was of a somewhat delicate constitution. Giulietta offered no resistance to this and went there.

In the belief that her father had sent her there so suddenly in order to hand her over without delay to her second husband, she took with her the powder which the friar had given her. That night close to four o'clock she called one of her handmaids who had been raised with her and whom she thus regarded as a sister, and had a goblet of cold water brought to her, saying she was thirsty because of the food she had eaten that evening; and once she had put the potent powder in it, she drank it all. Then, in the presence of her maid and one of her aunts who had awoken at the same time, she said: "My father will certainly not force me to take a husband if I can help it."

Although they had seen her drink the powder which she claimed to have put in the water so as to refresh herself, the two rather slow-witted women nevertheless did not understand what she meant and, unsuspecting, went back to sleep. With the lamp extinguished and her maid gone, Giulietta got out of bed and put all her clothes on again, pretending she was answering the call of nature. After she had returned to her bed, she composed herself on it as best she knew how, as though she believed she would die. With her hands crossed on her fair breast, she waited for the draught to take effect, which it did slightly more than two hours later, making her appear dead.

The next morning well after sunrise the maiden was found on the bed as I have described her. The aunt and chambermaid tried unsuccessfully to awaken her, but having found her already almost completely cold and recalling the water and powder she had drunk that night along with the words she had uttered, and on top of that seeing that she had dressed and arranged herself on the bed in that way, they believed beyond any doubt the powder to be poison and her to be dead.

A great outcry arose among the women, the weeping coming above all from the maid who, calling her mistress frequently by name, exclaimed: "Oh, my lady, this is what you were saying: 'My father will not force me to marry!' You misled me when asking for cold water, which was making ready your cruel death and my sorrow. Oh, wretch that I am, what should I weep for first? For your death or myself? Ah, why in dying did you scorn your servant's company which, when you were alive, you showed was so dear to you? For just as I have always lived willingly with you, so, too, would I have willingly died with you. Oh, my lady! I brought you the water with my own hands so that, wretch that I am, I might be abandoned by you in this way. I alone with one fell blow have killed you, myself, your father and your mother." Thus speaking, she climbed up onto the bed and tightly embraced the apparently dead maiden.

Messer Antonio, who from close by had heard the commotion, ran all atremble into his daughter's bedroom. Although he firmly believed her dead after seeing her on the bed and hearing what she had said and drunk that night, to be quite certain he promptly sent to Verona for a doctor of his whom he regarded as very learned and experienced. Having observed and summarily examined the maiden upon his arrival, the doctor pronounced that the poison she had consumed had caused her to pass from this life six hours earlier. At this, the wretched father began to weep most bitterly.

Passing from mouth to mouth, the sad news quickly reached the unhappy mother who, turning suddenly cold, fell as though dead. Once she had recovered her senses with a womanly cry, almost out of her mind she filled the heavens with her laments, striking herself all over, calling her beloved daughter by name and saying: "I behold you dead, oh my daughter, sole consolation of my old age! How could you have left me so cruelly without giving your wretched mother the chance to hear your last words? Would at least that it had been I who closed your beautiful eyes and washed your precious body! How can you do this to me? Oh, women most dear here before me, help me to die! And if you have any pity, let your hands rather than my own grief end my life, if such a task befits you. And you, great Father in heaven, strike me dead for I am hateful in my own eyes and cannot die as quickly as I would like!" And so, having been lifted onto her bed by some women and showered with comforting words by others, she did not leave off weeping and lamenting. Then the maiden was taken from there and transported to Verona where, with much pomp and honour, amidst the tears of all her relatives and friends she was buried as though dead in the aforementioned crypt in the cemetery of St Francis.

Frate Lorenzo, who had gone a short way from the city on monastery business, had given to a friar bound for Mantua the letter that Giulietta was to send to Romeo. This friar reached the city and, having been two or three times to Romeo's house without—unfortunately for him—ever finding him home, he still had the letter in his hand as he did not want to hand it over to anyone but him. At the same time Pietro, believing his mistress dead and not finding Frate

Lorenzo in Verona, near to despair decided to take in person to Romeo such news as he imagined the death of his wife must be to him. Thus after returning in the evening to the place outside the city where his master was, the following night he set out on foot for Mantua, arriving there early in the morning. Having found Romeo who had not yet received his wife's letter from the friar, he told him, weeping, of how he had seen the dead Giulietta buried and of all that she had done and said prior to that, omitting nothing.

On hearing this Romeo, deathly pale, wished to deal himself a mortal wound with his drawn sword but restrained by many, declared: "I shall not live much longer anyway since my only reason for living is dead. Oh, my Giulietta! I alone have caused your death[16] because I did not come to deliver you from your father, as I wrote that I would. You chose to die so as not to abandon me. Am I to go on living, alone, for fear of dying? This will never be!" Turning to Pietro and giving him a dark robe that he had on, he said: "Begone, Pietro my friend."

Once he had gone and Romeo had shut himself in alone, with all else appearing less wretched to him than life was, he gave much thought to what he should do with himself. Finally, dressed as a peasant and slipping into his sleeve a small phial of poison which, for a long time, he had kept safely in a box in case of need, he set out towards Verona, thinking to lose his life at the hands of justice, if he were found, or to shut himself up with his wife in the crypt, the location of which he knew very well, there to die.

Fortune so favoured this latter thought that the evening following the day of his wife's burial he entered Verona unrecognised. After waiting for nightfall and hearing nothing but silence all around, he headed towards the Church of the Friars Minor where the crypt was. This church was in the Citadel[17] in which these friars used to live at that time and although they thereafter left it (I know not why) to go and reside in the St Zeno area, now known as St Bernardino, still this church was named after St Francis. Near the outer side of the church walls there were then standing certain stone tombs such as we often see outside churches. One of these, in which the beautiful maid lay, was the old burial place of all the Capelletti.

Having approached it at what must have been around four o'clock and being the man of great strength that he was, Romeo succeeded in raising the cover of the tomb. After propping it up with some pieces of wood that he had brought with him so that it could not close unintentionally, he went into the tomb and closed it behind him. The unfortunate youth had brought with him a dark lantern[18] to enable him to behold his wife. Once enclosed in the crypt, he immediately took the lantern out and opened it. Amongst bones and the remains of many bodies he saw his beautiful Giulietta lying there as if dead. Thus he immediately began to lament, shedding copious tears: "Eyes, how dazzling you were to mine while it so pleased heaven! Oh, mouth, so sweetly kissed by mine a thousand times! Oh, beautiful breast, who harboured so joyfully my heart! How is it I now find you blind, dumb, and cold? How is it that I can see, speak, or live without you? Oh, my poor wife! Where have you been led by Love, who wills that so small a space should snuff out and enclose two wretched lovers? Alas! Other than this was I promised by that same hope and desire that first enflamed me with love for you. Oh, my cursed life, what sustains you?"

Thus speaking Romeo kissed her eyes, mouth and breast, lamenting through ever more copious tears. "Oh, walls above me, why do you not bring my life to an end more quickly by falling on me? But since death is within the reach of everyone, how base it is to desire it and yet not seize it!" Thus after taking out the phial containing the deadly poison that he had in his sleeve, he continued: "I know not what fate leads me to die on top of these enemies of mine whom I have slain and in their tomb, but since, oh my soul, it is fitting that we thus die near our lady, let us die forthwith." And having poured the lethal water into his mouth, he swallowed it all. Then taking the beloved maiden into his arms he said, embracing her tightly: "Oh, beautiful body, final object of all my desires, should any feeling remain in you now that your soul has departed or should your soul behold my cruel death, I pray that it not mind if at least I die in secret and full of woe as I was not able to live openly and happily with you." And clasping her tightly he awaited death.

The hour had already arrived when the maiden's warmth was supposed to have counteracted the cold and potent effect of the powder and she was to have awakened. Thus it was that, held tightly and shaken by Romeo, she awoke in his arms and, with her feelings restored, she uttered a deep sigh and the following words: "Alas, where am I? Who is holding me? Wretch that I am, who is kissing me?" And believing Frate Lorenzo responsible, she cried: "Is this how you show your loyalty to Romeo, friar? Is this how you intend leading me to safety?" Romeo was dumbfounded on hearing the woman and realising that she was alive; perhaps recalling Pygmalion,[19] he said: "Don't you recognise me, oh, my sweet wife? Can you not see that I am your wretched husband who has stolen back alone from Mantua to die at your side?"

On seeing herself in the crypt and feeling herself in the arms of someone who claimed to be Romeo, Giulietta was almost beside herself. After pushing him away from herself somewhat and examining his face, she kissed him countless times and said: "What folly made you place your life in danger by coming in here? Was it not enough for you to have learned from my letters how I, with Frate Lorenzo's help, was to feign death, and that soon I would be with you again?" Then realising his great error the wretched youth began to lament: "Oh, my most accursed fate! Oh, unfortunate Romeo, infinitely more sorrowful than all other lovers! Those letters of yours never reached me." He then explained to her how Pietro had told him of her apparent death as though it were real; wherefore, believing her dead, he had taken the poison here at her side so as to keep her company. Since this poison was lethal, he could already feel its deadly effects in all his limbs.

On hearing this, the ill-fated maiden was so overcome by grief that she knew not what to do besides tearing her beautiful hair and beating her innocent breast. Kissing again and again the already recumbent Romeo, she shed abundant tears over him and, having turned paler than ashes, she said all atremble: "Thus, my lord, because of me you must die here before me? And heaven will allow me to go on living, if only for a short time, after you are dead? Woe is me! If at least I could give you my life and die alone!" To which the youth replied weakly: "If my faithfulness and love were ever dear to you, my living hope, I beg you that life not displease you after I am gone, if for no other reason than you may at least think of him who, afire because of your beauty, is dying before your beautiful eyes." To this the woman replied: "If you die because of my apparent death, what ought I do if you really die? I regret only that I have no way of dying before you do and because I go on living, I am abhorrent to myself. But it is my fervent hope that, just as I was the cause of your death, so, before long, shall I be its companion." And after labouring to utter these words, she fell senseless. Once she had regained consciousness, with her lovely mouth she then set pitifully about capturing the last breath of her cherished lover who was rapidly approaching his end.

In the meantime Frate Lorenzo, who had learned how and when the maiden had drunk the powder and been buried as though dead, knowing that it was time the effects of the said powder began wearing off, came to the crypt with a trusted companion about an hour before daybreak. Arriving there and hearing her weeping and wailing, he peered between the lid and the crypt and saw a light inside. Greatly amazed, he concluded that the maiden had somehow taken the light in there with her and that, after awaking, she was lamenting and weeping thus out of fear of some dead body or perhaps of remaining shut in that place for ever. With the help of his companion he promptly opened the tomb and saw Giulietta who, dishevelled and grief-stricken, had sat up and gathered her near-dead lover into her lap. Addressing her, he said: "So, my daughter, you feared that I would leave you to die in here?" Hearing the friar and weeping twice as much, she answered: "On the contrary, I fear you may take me out alive. Ah, for pity's sake, close the tomb up again and begone so that I may die. Or else hand me a knife so that by wounding myself in the breast I may put an end to my grief. Oh, father, father, how well you sent the letter! How well shall I be wed! How well you will lead me to Romeo! Behold him here already dead in my lap." And telling him all that had happened, she showed him Romeo.

On hearing these things, Frate Lorenzo appeared stunned and gazing at the youth who was about to pass from this life into the next, spoke thus: "Oh, Romeo, what dire misfortune has taken you from me? Say something to me, look at me a moment! Oh, Romeo, see your beloved Giulietta who begs you to look at her! Why don't you at least answer her in whose lovely lap you are lying?" At the dear name of his wife Romeo raised briefly eyes made dim and heavy by approaching death and, after seeing her, closed them again. Shortly thereafter, with death coursing through his writhing limbs, he gave a short sigh and died.

Once the wretched lover had died in the way I have described to you, following much weeping the friar said to the maid as day was already drawing near: "And you, Giulietta, what will you do?" She promptly replied: "I shall die in here." "What? My daughter," he said, "don't say this. Come on out, for even though I do not know what to do with you, you can always shut yourself away in some holy convent, ever praying to God on your own behalf as well as that of your dead husband, if he has need of it." To which the woman replied: "Father, I ask nothing else of you but this favour which, for the love that you bore his happy memory"—and she indicated Romeo—"you will willingly do for me: and this is that you never make known our death, so that our bodies may remain together for ever in this tomb. And if by chance our death should become known, I beg you in the name of this same love to entreat our unfortunate fathers on both our behalves that it not displease them to leave in the same tomb those whom Love burned in the same fire and led to the same death."

Having turned to the reclining body of Romeo, whose head she had placed on a pillow that had been left in the crypt with her, and having closed his eyes completely Giulietta said while bathing his cold face with tears: "What am I supposed to do, my lord, now that you are no longer alive? What else is left for me where you are concerned, except to join you in death? Nothing else to be sure, in order that death may not separate me from you, as only it was able to do." Having spoken thus, she focused her mind on her great misfortune; recalling the loss of her dear lover and resolving to live no longer, she drew in her breath, held it for some time, then letting it out with a great cry she fell lifeless on the dead body of Romeo.

Realising that the maiden was dead and overwhelmed with pity, Frate Lorenzo himself was undecided what to do. Together with his companion, he was weeping over the dead lovers from heart-felt grief when the *podestà*'s[20] guards, who were chasing after some thief, happened by there. Having found them weeping over this tomb in which they could see a lantern, almost to a man they hastened there and, surrounding the two friars, asked: "What are you doing here at this hour, reverend fathers? Would you perhaps be practising sorcery over this crypt?" Having seen, heard and recognised these officials, Frate Lorenzo would have preferred to be dead, yet he said to them: "Don't any one of you come near since you cannot arrest me;[21] and if you want anything, ask from a distance." Their leader then said: "We want to know why you have opened the Capelletti tomb like that, wherein just the day before yesterday one of their young women was buried; and if I didn't know you for a man of good standing, Frate Lorenzo, I would say that you had come here to rob the dead." After extinguishing the light, the friars replied: "You won't learn what we are doing because it's no concern of yours." The same guard replied: "This is true, but I shall tell the city lord." To which Frate

Lorenzo added, made bold by desperation: "Say what you wish"; and after securing the tomb, he went into the church with his companion.

It was almost broad daylight when the friars got free of the guards. One of them immediately reported the news of these friars to several of the Capelletti who, realising perhaps that Frate Lorenzo was still on friendly terms with Romeo, promptly appeared before the city lord, begging him to find out from the friar, if not otherwise then by force, what he had been up to in the tomb. After he had posted guards to prevent the friar from leaving, the city lord sent for him. Once the friar had been brought before him by force, the lord said: "What were you looking for this morning in the Capelletti tomb? Tell us, because we intend to know it at all costs." To this the friar replied: "My lord, I shall tell you most willingly. While she was still alive, I heard the confession of Messer Antonio Capelletti's daughter, who died so strangely the other day. Since I loved her dearly as a devout daughter and was unable to attend her funeral service, I had gone to say some special prayers for her which, when repeated nine times over the body, free the soul from the pains of purgatory. As few people know or understand these things, the ignorant say that I had gone there to rob the dead. I am certainly no grave-robber to do things like that; this frock and cord are all I need. I care nothing at all for the wealth of the living and even less for the clothing of two dead people. They do wrong who thus accuse me."

The lord would easily have believed this if many friars, who bore Frate Lorenzo ill-will, had not insisted on opening that tomb on learning how he had been found near it. Once it had been opened and the body of the dead lover found in it, the city lord, who was still conversing with the friar, was immediately told amongst much commotion that Romeo Montecchi was lying dead in the Capelletti tomb near which the friar had been caught the previous night. To all present this seemed almost impossible and caused great astonishment. Upon hearing this and realising he could no longer keep hidden what he would have liked to, Frate Lorenzo went down on his knees before the lord and said: "Forgive me, my lord, if I lied to your lordship in response to what you asked me. This I did not out of malice nor for any personal gain but to keep the promise I made two poor, dead lovers." Thus he was compelled to tell him the whole story before a large gathering.

Almost moved to tears by great pity on hearing this, Bartolomeo della Scala wanted to see the bodies himself and went to the tomb with a large crowd of people. After having the lovers removed, he had them placed on two rugs inside the Church of St Francis. Meanwhile, their fathers came to the said church and, weeping over their dead children, overcome by pity on two counts they embraced one another even though they were enemies. Thus the long-standing enmity between them and their families, which neither the pleading of friends, nor the lord's threats, nor injuries received, nor time had been able to extinguish, came to an end because of the unfortunate and pitiful death of these lovers. And after a beautiful monument was ordered on which the cause of their death was engraved within a few days, the two lovers, accompanied and mourned by the lord, relatives and the entire city, were buried with great and solemn pomp. Such was the unhappy end of the love of Romeo and Giulietta, as you have heard and as Peregrino from Verona related it to me.

Oh, faithful compassion that reigned in women in times gone by, where have you gone? In what breast do you dwell to-day? What present-day woman would have died next to her lover as faithful Giulietta did? When will her fair name be celebrated by the most able tongues? How many women nowadays, as soon as they had seen their lover dead, would have thought of finding another rather than dying next to him? Because if I see some women, oblivious to all reason, faithfulness and loyalty, desert lovers formerly very dear to them who don't die but are simply mistreated by fortune, what are we to believe they would do once their lovers were dead? Wretched present-day lovers! Neither by serving their ladies long and faithfully nor by dying for them can such lovers hope that their ladies will ever die with them. As a matter of fact, some lovers are appreciated by their ladies only in proportion to the vigour with which they satisfy their needs.

Here ends the star-crossed love of Romeo Montecchi and Giulietta Capelletti.

# *Matteo Bandello*

"La sfortunata morte di dui infelicissimi amanti che l'uno di veleno e l'altro di dolore morirono, con vari accidenti." (*Novelle*, Part II, novella 9)

*Bandello to the most magnificent and excellent Messer Girolamo Fracastoro,*[22] *poet and most learned doctor, greetings.*

This summer that most worthy and illustrious gentleman Cesare Fregoso,[23] your very good friend and my lord, went to drink the waters of the spa at Caldiero[24] where he was a guest in the house of Messer Matteo Boldiero, a most courteous person, temperate and beyond reproach in every aspect of his life. As you know much better than I do, many people converge there from all over Lombardy, Germany and other parts both near and far for the benefits offered by the waters, the marvellous effects of which are seen whenever they are drunk as prescribed. I, amongst others, can personally vouch for this, for when I was severely afflicted with an irksome kidney complaint, you sent daily to Caldiero for these waters and had me drink them here in Verona for several days. The benefit that I derived from them was such as both you and I were hoping for; the pain disappeared completely and I have not felt so much as a twinge since, whereas before I could not bend down or straighten up without acute pain.

Signor Cesare remained at this spa for quite a few days, taking advantage of the decorous freedom granted to those partaking of the waters, enjoying himself at the spa in the company of others like himself. From the surrounding cities many gentlemen came to visit him, all of whom he gladly received and honoured at table with abundant, sumptuous fare, for well you know how he honours those whom he thinks worthy of it. There were various pleasant pastimes, and all present devoted themselves to the activity that afforded them most pleasure.

One day during a discussion concerning the havoc that love can cause, Captain Alessandro Peregrino recounted a pitiful story which took place in Verona when Bartolomeo Scala[25] was lord and which, thanks to its unhappy outcome, caused almost all of us to weep. And because I thought it worthy of compassion and of being consecrated to posterity, I wrote it down as a warning to the young to act with restraint rather than rashness. Thus I present to you my written version of that story, knowing from experience that you welcome my nonsense and read it willingly; the learned and harmonious epigram that my *Parche* prompted you to write[26] clearly shows this to be so. Good health.

*The unfortunate death of two most wretched lovers, one of whom died of poison, the other, of grief; and various other unhappy events.*

I believe, my worthy lord, if the affection which I rightly bear my native city deceives me not,[27] that few are the cities of beautiful Italy which can surpass in beauty the setting of Verona, with its noble river, the Adige, whose crystal clear waters divide the city almost in half while enriching it with the merchandise that Germany sends, and the delightful, fertile hills and pleasant valleys with their sunny fields that surround it. I shan't dwell on the many fountains that provide the city abundantly with the freshest, clearest water, on the four majestic bridges spanning the river, on the countless glorious monuments to be seen everywhere. But because I did not set out to praise my birthplace, the attractions of which speak for themselves, I shall tell you of the great and pitiful misfortune that there befell two most noble lovers.

At the time when Verona was under the rule of the Della Scala, two families lived there, very famous amongst others for their nobility and wealth. They were the Montecchi and the Capelletti, both influential families who were embroiled for some reason or other in a fierce and bloody feud that had resulted in many Montecchi and Capelletti alike, along with their supporters, losing their lives in sundry brawls, which served to increase their hatred. At that time the lord of Verona was Bartolomeo Scala who did his utmost to reconcile these two houses but without success, so deeply rooted was the hatred in their hearts. However, he influenced them to the extent that, if he did not establish peace between them, at least he eliminated the constant brawls that very frequently broke out between them causing the loss of lives. Thus if they ran into each other on the street, the young gave way to the older members of the opposite faction.

It happened then one year after Christmas that masquerades began to be held at which masked guests gathered together. Antonio Capelletti, the head of his family, gave a most delightful party to which he invited a great gathering of noble men and women. Most of the city's young people were to be seen there, including Romeo Montecchi, not yet twenty-one years of age, the most handsome and well-mannered youth in all of Verona. He was masked and entered the Capelletti house with the others after night had already fallen.

Romeo at that time was madly in love with a lady at whose mercy he had placed himself some two years earlier, and although all day long he always followed her to churches or wherever else she went, nonetheless she had never granted him the courtesy of a single glance. He had repeatedly written her letters and sent messengers, but such was the unshakeable resolve of the woman that she did not even deign to give the impassioned youth a kindly look. This was so grievous and difficult for him to bear that, because of the extreme pain he suffered and after a great deal of lamentation, he resolved to abandon Verona for a year or two, curbing this unrestrained craving of his by travelling around Italy.

Overcome then by the ardent love he bore her, he berated himself for having entertained such an insane thought and was quite incapable of leaving. At times he would say to himself: "May it not be true that I love her any longer, since I know beyond all doubt from a thousand signs that she does not hold my servitude dear. Why follow her wherever she goes, if loving her from afar avails me naught? I would do better not to go to church or anywhere else she may be, because if I do not see her, perhaps this fire of mine that is kindled and fuelled by her beautiful eyes will gradually die down."

Vain hope! All his thoughts turned out to be futile because it seemed that the more she appeared reluctant and the less hope he had, the more his love for her grew, and that the days when he did not see her were a torment to him. And as he remained unshakeably steadfast and ardent in this love of his, several of his friends, fearing that he would pine away, lovingly warned him many times, entreating him to withdraw from such an undertaking. But he paid as much attention to their sincere warnings and salutary advice as the woman did to him.

Amongst Romeo's friends there was one in particular who very much regretted seeing Romeo waste the best years of his youth running after this woman without hope of any reward. Thus he spoke to him as he had done many times before: "Romeo, loving you like a brother as I do, it troubles me greatly to see you waste away in this way like snow in the sun; and since you can see that with all you do and spend—and your spending is repaid with neither honour nor profit—you can't make her condescend to love you, and that whatever means you employ not only proves ineffectual but rather increases her reluctance, why do you weary yourself in vain? To wish for something that is not merely difficult but beyond reach is pure folly. You have had ample proof that she cares nothing for you nor for what concerns you. Perhaps she has some lover so pleasing and dear to her that she would not give him up for anyone in the world. You are young, perhaps the most handsome youth to be found in this city of ours. You are, if I may be permitted to speak truthfully to your face, well-mannered, virtuous, lovable and, something which greatly enhances youth, graced with learning. Moreover, you are your father's only son, and his wealth is well known to everyone. Is he perhaps tight-fisted with you or remonstrates if you spend and bestow money as you see fit? All his industry and hard work are for your sake, and he lets you do what you want. Wake up and recognise the illusion under which you have been labouring! Take away the veil that blinds your eyes and prevents you from seeing the path you ought to tread! Make up your mind to turn your thoughts elsewhere and to make mistress of your heart a woman who is worthy of it. May you be stirred by rightful contempt, which can accomplish much more in the realm of love than love itself can. Festivities and masquerades are beginning to be held all over the city: go to all of them, and if by chance you see there she whom you have served so long in vain, gaze not at her but reflect on the love that you have borne her, and without doubt you will find a cure for the ill you suffer, because there will be kindled within you such right and proper contempt as will curb this unrestrained craving of yours and set you free."

Using many other reasoned arguments that I will not go into now, Romeo's faithful companion urged him to withdraw from an enterprise that he should never have begun. Romeo listened patiently to what was said to him and resolved to put the sound advice into action. Thus he began attending festivities and he never cast his eyes where he knew the reluctant woman to be, but rather looked appraisingly at the other women to select the one that pleased him most, as if he had gone to a market to buy horses or cloth.

It happened one day, as has already been said, that Romeo went in costume to the Capelletti party and although there was little friendship between them, they did not insult one another. After Romeo had been there some time with a mask covering his face, he removed it and withdrew to sit in a corner from where he could easily see everyone in the room which, lit as it was by many torches, was as bright as if it had been day. Everyone was looking at Romeo, particularly the women, and all were amazed that he should dally so openly in that house. Nevertheless, because Romeo was not only very handsome but a well-mannered and courteous young man as well, he was loved by most people. His enemies did not give as much thought to him as they would have done had he been older. Romeo set himself up there as judge of the beauty of the women present at the party, and praised in varying degrees this woman and that according to the desire they aroused in him.

He was keeping himself thus entertained without dancing when an indescribably lovely maiden whom he did not know caught his attention. The sight of her gave him immeasurable pleasure and he deemed her to be the most beautiful and charming young woman he had ever seen. It seemed to Romeo that the more intently he gazed at her, the more her beauty and charms increased. Thus he began to look upon her most amorously, unable to take his eyes off her. Since looking at her aroused such unaccustomed joy in him, he resolved to make every effort to gain her favour and love. Thus it was that the love he bore the other woman, vanquished by the new love, gave way to such flames as only death thereafter would extinguish.

Once Romeo had entered this alluring labyrinth, lacking the courage to find out who the young woman was, he feasted his eyes on the captivating sight of her and, giving his close attention to all she did, he drank love's sweet poison, awed by her every attribute and gesture. As I have already said, he was sitting in a corner in front of which all passed when they were dancing. Giulietta—for this was the name of the maiden that Romeo liked so much—was the daughter of the owner of the house whose party it was. Although she did not yet know Romeo, still he seemed to her the most handsome and charming youth that one could encounter. She found wondrous satisfaction in looking, and stealing every now and then sweet and furtive glances at him, she felt I know not what sweetness in her heart that overwhelmed her with joyful and extreme pleasure. The maiden longed for Romeo to begin dancing so that she could see him better and hear him speak, seeming as it did to her that the sweetness of his speech must equal that from his eyes which she appeared to enjoy so immeasurably while she went on looking at him. But he remained seated all by himself, and showed no inclination to dance.

He was wholly intent upon gazing in admiration at the beautiful young maid and she had no other thought but to look at him. They were looking at one another in such a way that, with their eyes at times meeting and their ardent glances uniting, they readily realised that their gazes were amorous. Thus every time their eyes met, both filled the air with amorous sighs and it appeared that, for the time being, they desired nothing more than to be able to disclose their newly-kindled flame by talking to one another.

With both of them now lost in this fond contemplation, the dancing festivities came to an end and the dance of the torch began, which others call the dance of the hat.[28] While this amusement was underway, Romeo, who was invited to join the dance by a woman, joined in and did what was expected of him. Having given the torch to a woman, he went close to Giulietta as the rules of the dance demanded and took her by the hand, to the boundless pleasure of both concerned. Giulietta had ended up between Romeo and someone known as Marcuccio the Cross-Eyed, a very pleasant courtier generally well regarded for his capacity for light-hearted witticisms and pleasantries. Hence he always had some anecdote at the ready to make the company laugh, and he would amuse himself most willingly without causing offence to anyone. In all weather and seasons, his hands were always much colder and frozen than the coldest alpine ice, and although he stayed by the fire warming them at length, nevertheless they remained icy cold.

As Giulietta—who had Romeo on her left and Marcuccio on her right—felt her beloved take her hand, she turned slightly towards him, perhaps eager to hear him speak, and said with a happy expression and trembling voice: “Blessed be your arrival at my side!”;

and thus saying, she squeezed his hand lovingly. The astute youth, who was nobody's fool, answered her thus while gently squeezing her hand: "My lady, what does this blessing of yours mean?"; and looking at her beseechingly, he hung on her answer, sighing. Laughing sweetly, she then answered: "Do not be amazed, kind young sir, if I bless your coming here, for Messer Marcuccio has for some time been freezing me all over with the chill of his cold hand and you mercifully warm me with your soft hand." To this Romeo immediately added: "My lady, it means a great deal to me that I am able to do you some service, and I yearn for nothing else in the world other than to be able to serve you. Hence I shall consider myself blessed whenever you deign to command me as you would your humblest servant. I can truly say that if my hand warms you, with the fire of your beautiful eyes you make me burn all over, ensuring that if you deny me help so that I can withstand such a fire, it will not be long before you see me burn up and turn to ashes."

No sooner was he able to finish saying these last words than the game of the torch came to an end. Thus Giulietta, who was burning with love, had no time to give him any answer other than to say, sighing and squeezing his hand: "Alas, what can I say to you if not that I belong far more to you than I do to myself?" Since everyone was leaving, Romeo waited to see in which direction the young maid would head; but it was not long before he knew beyond any doubt that she was the daughter of the master of the house, and he also sought verification of this by inquiring of a well-wisher of his about many women. This aggrieved him greatly, believing as he did that to achieve the desired outcome of this love of his would be a difficult and dangerous enterprise. But the wound was already open and love's poison had gone deep.

On the other hand Giulietta, eager to know the identity of the youth in whose power she already felt herself wholly to be, after summoning her old wet-nurse entered a room, went to a window lit up by many torches blazing in the street, and began asking her who so-and-so was wearing such-and-such an outfit, who was this one and that other carrying a sword. She also inquired of her the identity of the handsome youth holding the mask in his hand. The kindly old woman, who knew almost everybody, named first one and then the other, and knowing Romeo very well, told Giulietta who he was. On hearing the Montecchi name the maiden was stunned, despairing of ever being able to have Romeo as her husband because of the hostile rivalry between their two families; nonetheless she allowed no sign of her despair to show.

After retiring then for the night she slept little or not at all, turning over various thoughts in her head; but she was neither willing nor able to cease loving her Romeo, so ardent was her love for him. And being swayed by her lover's incredible beauty, the more difficult and dangerous she perceived her situation to be, the more her desire appeared to increase as her hope diminished. Thus prey to two conflicting thoughts, one of which gave her courage to pursue her intent while the other denied her all access to it, she repeated over and over to herself: "Where am I allowing myself to be led by my wayward desires? How do I know, fool that I am, that Romeo loves me? Perhaps the cunning youth said what he did to deceive me, so that by obtaining from me something unbefitting my virtue he can make fun of me and turn me into a woman of ill repute, perhaps thinking by so doing to take revenge for the ever-worsening enmity between his relatives and mine. But he is not so lacking in kindness as to be able to deceive she who loves and worships him. If his face is a clear indication of his thoughts, then beauty as alluring as his harbours beneath it no such hard and merciless heart; but rather I prefer to think that nothing except love, courtesy, and gentility can be expected from such a courteous and handsome youth."

"Now let us suppose," she went on, "that he really loves me and wants me for his lawful wife, as I am inclined to believe: ought I not reasonably assume that my father will never consent to it? But who knows if it is not possible to hope that this marriage will bring continuing harmony and lasting peace between these two families? I have often heard it said that marriages have brought peace not only between private citizens and noblemen, but that to the satisfaction of all concerned true peace and friendship have ensued many times between great princes and kings once divided by bloody wars. Perhaps through this event I shall be the one to restore peace to these two families." And holding fast to this idea, she never hid her happiness from Romeo whenever she saw him pass by that way, which caused him great pleasure.

Although Romeo's mental turmoil was no less than Giulietta's, alternating as he did between hope and despair, he nevertheless persisted in walking past the beloved maiden's house both by day and night, to his great peril. But Giulietta's benevolent glances, enflaming him more and more, drew him to that area. The windows of Giulietta's room were above a very narrow alley opposite which there was an abandoned house. When Romeo arrived at the beginning of the alley on his way along the main street, he would often see the young woman at the window and whenever he did, her expression was welcoming, indicating her pleasure at seeing him. Romeo often went there at night and stopped in the alley, both because that street was not used and because by standing opposite the window he sometimes heard his beloved talk.

It so happened that while he was there one night, either Giulietta heard him or for some other reason she opened the window. Romeo took cover inside the abandoned house, but not before she had recognised him, since moonlight was lighting up the alley. Being alone in her room, she called him softly and said: "Romeo, what are you doing here all alone at this hour? Woe if you were caught there! What would become of you? Are you not aware of the cruel feud existing between members of your family and ours and how many have already died because of it? Without doubt you would be cruelly slain, which for you would mean disaster and for me, dishonour."

"My lady," Romeo replied, "the love which I bear you is the reason for my coming here at this time, and I have no doubt whatsoever that if your kinsmen were to find me here they would seek to kill me. But for what my feeble strength is worth, I would strive to do my duty, and should I see myself overcome by powers greater than my own, I would do my best not to die alone. And as I am to die anyway in this amorous quest, what more fortunate death can befall me than to die close to you? That I should ever be responsible to even the smallest degree for staining your honour, I do not believe will ever happen, because I would give my own blood in order to preserve the purity and renown of your reputation. But if your love for me were as powerful as mine is for you, and if you cared as much about my life as I do about yours, you would eliminate the need for risk and take the necessary steps to make me the happiest man alive to-day." "And what would you have me do?" asked Giulietta. "I would wish that you loved me," Romeo answered, "as I love you, and that you let me come into your room so that with greater ease and less danger I might reveal to you the extent of my love and the bitter pains I constantly suffer for you."

Somewhat angered and upset, Giulietta replied: "Romeo, you know the extent of your love as I do of mine, and I know that I love you as much as it is possible to love anyone and perhaps more than befits my honour. But let me assure you that if you think to take your pleasure of me prior to the fitting bond of matrimony, you are gravely mistaken and we will never be of one mind. And because I know that by frequenting this neighbourhood too often you could easily run into trouble and I would nevermore be happy, if you wish to be mine as I long to be ever yours I decree that you should take me as your lawful wife. If you wed me, I shall always be prepared to follow you wherever you see fit to go. If you have some other fancy in mind, be on your way and let me live in peace as I please."

On hearing these words Romeo, who yearned for nothing else, happily replied that this was his sole desire and that he would wed her in whatever way she commanded whenever it pleased her. "So be it," Giulietta added, "but so that our affairs are carried out properly, I would like our marriage to be celebrated in the presence of the reverend Frate Lorenzo from Reggio, my spiritual father." They agreed on this and it was arranged that Romeo would talk to him about the matter the following day, being, as he was, on close terms with him.

Frate Lorenzo of the Friars Minor was a master in theology, an expert in natural science, skilled at distilling wondrous potions and well versed in the art of magic. Since the good friar wished to remain in the good graces of the common people while still indulging in his chosen pursuits, he made every effort to go about his business as discreetly as possible, always seeking the support of some esteemed noble person as a precautionary measure. Amongst these friends of his in Verona who showed him favour there was Romeo's father, a nobleman of great repute highly regarded by everyone, who firmly believed the friar to be most devout. Romeo likewise loved him very much and was in turn greatly loved by the friar who knew him to be a youth both prudent and brave. Not only was he a frequent guest in the Montecchi house, but he was also on very familiar terms with the Capelletti; moreover, he heard the confession of most of the city's nobles, men and women alike.

Once Romeo had thus bid farewell to Giulietta mindful of the above-mentioned plan, he left her and went home. The next day he went to the Church of St Francis and told the friar all about his love and the decision he and Giulietta had made. When Frate Lorenzo heard this he promised to do all that Romeo wanted, both because he could deny him nothing and also because in this way he was convinced he could end the feud between the Capelletti and

Montecchi, thus ingratiating himself even more with Lord Bartolomeo, who desired nothing more than that these two houses should be reconciled so that peace could be restored to his city.

The two lovers were waiting for an opportunity to have their confession heard so they could carry out their plan when Lent began. As an added precaution, Giulietta decided to take into her confidence an old servant of hers who slept in the same room as she did and, seizing the opportunity, she divulged the whole story of her love to the worthy dame, who scolded Giulietta soundly and advised her against such a venture; but to no avail. Giulietta was so persuasive that the old woman bowed to her will, agreeing to take a letter to Romeo who, on reading it, was the happiest man in the world as Giulietta had written that at the fifth hour of the night he was to come and talk at the window opposite the abandoned house and bring with him a rope ladder.

Romeo had a very reliable servant whom he had trusted a number of times in matters of great importance and had always found him willing and loyal. Having told him what he intended doing, to him Romeo gave the task of finding the rope ladder and, having organised everything, at the appointed hour he went with Pietro—for this was the servant's name—to the place where he found Giulietta waiting for him. When she recognised him she let down the string that she had ready and pulled up the ladder attached to it. Helped by the old woman who was with her, with the ladder securely fixed to the grating she waited for her lover to climb up, which he boldly did and Pietro took cover in the abandoned house.

Once Romeo had climbed up to the window with its grating so thick and strong that only with difficulty could a hand pass through it, he began talking with Giulietta who, after they had exchanged loving greetings, spoke thus to her lover: "My lord, dearer to me by far than light is to my eyes, I have summoned you here because I have arranged with my mother that I shall go to confession this coming Friday at sermon time. Let Frate Lorenzo know so that he can take care of everything." Romeo replied that the friar had been informed and was prepared to do what they wanted. After they had spoken together at length about their love, when it seemed to them timely Romeo climbed down, detached the ladder from the cord and, together with Pietro, departed with it.

Giulietta was so overjoyed at the thought of marrying Romeo that an hour seemed like centuries. Romeo for his part could not contain his joy as he spoke with his servant. When the Friday arrived Giulietta's mother, Madonna Giovanna, accompanied by her daughter and the women of the house, went as planned to the Church of St Francis, then located in the Citadel, and once inside had Frate Lorenzo summoned. The friar, who was privy to everything and had already admitted Romeo into the cell from which he carried out confessions and had locked him in, came to the woman who said to him: "Father, I have come to confession early and have brought Giulietta with me because I know that you will be very busy all day hearing the confessions of your spiritual children."

Having blessed them in the name of God, the friar went into the convent and entered the confessional where Romeo was. On the other side, Giulietta was the first to come before the reverend friar. After entering the confessional and closing the door she gave the friar the sign that she was in there. He removed the grate and, after the proper greetings, said to Giulietta: "My daughter, according to what Romeo tells me, you have agreed to take him as your husband and he is willing to take you as his wife. Are you both still of the same mind?" The lovers replied that this was their sole desire. Once the reverend friar had heard their mutual resolve, he spoke briefly in praise of holy matrimony and pronounced the words customary within the Church for wedding ceremonies. Romeo gave the ring to his beloved Giulietta, to the great pleasure of both. After Romeo had arranged to visit Giulietta the following night and they had kissed one another through the small opening of the window, Romeo cautiously left first the cell and then the convent and happily went about his business. Once the friar had replaced the grate in the window in such a way that no one could notice that it had been removed, he heard first the confession of the happy maiden and then that of her mother and the other women.

After nightfall, at the appointed time Romeo went with Pietro to a certain garden wall which he climbed with the servant's help, then lowering himself into the garden where he found his wife and her elderly servant waiting for him. When he saw Giulietta, he went to meet her with his arms open. Giulietta did the same, and she remained clinging to his neck for some time, overwhelmed by such sweetness that she could not utter a word. Her enflamed lover was likewise affected, seeming as it did to him that he had never experienced such pleasure. They then began to kiss each other, to the boundless pleasure and indescribable joy of both concerned. Having then withdrawn to a corner of the garden, by lying together in love on some bench that was there they consummated their holy marriage. As Romeo was a young man of considerable stamina and very much in love, he repeatedly took pleasure of his beautiful bride. Then after arranging to meet again and, in the meantime, to begin negotiations with Messer Antonio for peace to be restored and their kinship accepted, Romeo kissd his wife countless times and left the garden, saying joyfully to himself: "What man is there alive today in this world who is happier than I? What man can possibly be my equal in love? Who ever had such a beautiful and fair young maiden as I have?" Giulietta was no less delighted and considered herself no less blessed, imagining as she did that it would be impossible to find another youth who was Romeo's equal in good looks, fine manners, courtesy, gentility and a thousand other endearing, beautiful endowments. Thus it was with the greatest desire in the world that she waited for circumstances to change so that she could take pleasure in Romeo without fear.

Thus it happened that the newly-weds met some days and others they did not. Frate Lorenzo in the meantime was doing what he could to restore peace between the Montecchi and Capelletti and he had progressed so well in the negotiations that he had every hope of settling the matter of the lovers' marriage to the complete satisfaction of both parties.

During the Resurrection festivities at Easter it happened, on the Corso near the Gate of the Borsari going towards Castelvecchio, that a large group of Capelletti ran into several Montecchi and attacked them boldly with weapons. Amongst the Capelletti was Tebaldo, Giulietta's cousin, a very audacious youth who urged his kinsmen to strike the Montecchi boldly and dispassionately. The fight was escalating and, with reinforcements and arms all the while coming to the aid of both sides, the brawlers were becoming so heated that they were exchanging wounds indiscriminately.

As chance would have it Romeo, accompanied not only by his servants but also by several young companions, turned up as they were strolling around the city. When he saw that the Capelletti were laying hands on his kinsmen he became very upset because, knowing the peace negotiations being conducted by the friar, he wanted no quarrels to take place. In order to restore quiet, he said loudly to his companions and servants, overheard by many others in the street: "Brothers, let us intervene and in some way or other see to it that the brawl does not continue, doing our best to make them lay down their arms." Thus he began to drive his own and the other men back and, followed by his companions, with his deeds and words he strove valiantly to prevent the brawl from proceeding further. But he could do nothing, as the fury of both parties had so increased that all they could think about was fighting.

Two or three from both sides had already fallen to the ground and Romeo had tried in vain to make his men draw back when Tebaldo approached furtively and delivered Romeo a forceful blow to the side. But because Romeo was wearing a coat of mail he was not wounded since the rapier could not penetrate his cuirass. Thus turned towards Tebaldo he addressed him as a friend: "You are very much mistaken, Tebaldo, if you believe that I have come here to quarrel with you or your kinsmen. I happened here by chance and intervened to take my men away, prompted by the desire that from now on we might live together as good citizens. And I urge and pray you to do likewise with yours to avoid further outcry, because already too much blood has been spilt." These words were heard by almost everyone, but Tebaldo either did not hear what Romeo said or pretended not to and replied: "Ah, death to you, traitor!", and he flung himself at him with fury to wound him in the head. Romeo as always was wearing sleeve of mail, and with his cloak wound around his left arm, he raised it above his head and, by deflecting the tip of the sword towards his enemy, wounded him directly in the throat, running the sword through, so that Tebaldo immediately collapsed face downwards to the ground, dead.

A great outcry arose and with the arrival of the court bodyguards, the fighters fled in all directions. Overcome with grief at having killed Tebaldo, Romeo fled in the company of many of his kinsmen to the Church of St Francis where he took refuge in Frate Lorenzo's room. Hearing how young Tebaldo had died the good friar was in despair, believing that there was no longer any way to resolve the feud between the two families. All the Capelletti appeared together before Lord Bartolomeo to lay a formal complaint. On the Montecchi side, the father of the concealed Romeo backed up by the other family elders established that Romeo, while strolling around the city with his friends, had turned up by chance where the Montecchi had been set upon by the Capelletti, and had joined in the brawl to prevent scandal and restore quiet. They explained how Romeo, treacherously wounded by Tebaldo, had begged him to make his men withdraw and lay down their arms, and how Tebaldo had attempted to wound him a second time, and with what outcome. And thus with both sides exchanging accusations and accepting no blame, they waged a heated dispute before Lord Bartolomeo. However, as it was blatantly obvious that the Capelletti had been the aggressors, after many trustworthy witnesses had substantiated what Romeo had said first to his companions and then to Tebaldo, Lord Bartolomeo sentenced Romeo to exile after ordering everyone to lay down arms.

There was great lamenting in the Capelletti house over the death of Tebaldo. Giulietta gave herself over to an incessant flood of bitter tears, caused not by the death of her cousin but by the loss of all hope for her marriage. For this reason she was overwhelmed with sadness and grieved woefully, unable to imagine how the matter would end. Having then heard from Frate Lorenzo where Romeo was, she wrote him a tearful letter which she sent to the friar by means of the dame.

Giulietta knew that Romeo had been banished and had to leave Verona, hence she entreated him most lovingly to allow her to leave with him. Romeo wrote back that she should resign herself to the situation because in time he would see to everything; that although he had not yet made up his mind where he ought to take refuge, it would be as close as possible; and that before he left he would make every effort to meet with her in person to talk wherever was more convenient for her. She chose as the least dangerous place the garden in which her marriage had been consummated, and once the exact night they were to meet had been determined, with the help of Frate Lorenzo Romeo left the convent armed and went to his wife, accompanied by his ever-faithful Pietro.

Once he was inside the garden, Giulietta greeted him weeping countless tears. They both remained for some time unable to say a word, drinking in the abundant tears which both were shedding as they kissed. Then bemoaning the fact that they had to be separated so soon, all they could do was weep and lament their star-crossed love, and embracing and kissing, several times they took amorous pleasure of one another.

As the time drew near for them to leave one another, Giulietta pleaded with her husband as fervently as she knew how to take her with him. "My dear lord," she said, "I shall cut my long hair short and dress as a boy, and wherever you see fit to go, I shall always come with you and serve you lovingly. And what more faithful servant than me could you have? Ah, my dear husband, grant me this favour and let me share the same fate as you so that what befalls you, befalls me too."

Romeo comforted her as best he could with sweet words, doing his utmost to console her and assuring her of his conviction that his banishment would soon be revoked, as the prince had already given some hope of this to his father. He explained that when he saw fit to take her with him, he would take her not dressed as a page but rather he would want her to accompany him honourably as his wife, lady and equal. He then declared that the banishment would not last more than a year, because if in the meantime peace was not made amicably between their relatives, then the lord would take the matter in hand, compelling them to make peace despite any opposition there might be. Whatever happened, if he saw that things were dragging on too long he would think of something else, it being impossible for him to live without her for any great length of time. They agreed then to keep in touch by letter. Romeo uttered many words of consolation to his wife before leaving her but the disconsolate young woman did nothing but weep. Finally, as dawn was beginning to break the lovers kissed and embraced tightly, then bid each other farewell through their copious tears and sighs. Romeo returned to the Church of St Francis, Giulietta to her room.

Two or three days later Romeo, having already planned his departure, slipped out of Verona under cover dressed as a foreign merchant. He found a group of good and trusted companions at the ready and journeyed to Mantua in safety. There he took a house and lived in honour and good company, as his father did not make him want for money. All day long Giulietta did nothing else but weep and sigh, eating little and sleeping less; and nights were no different. When Giulietta's mother saw her daughter weeping, she asked her time and time again what the matter was and why she was so unhappy, saying that the time had come for her to stop crying as she had already wept too much over the death of her cousin. Giulietta would reply that she did not know what the matter was. Yet whenever she was able to slip away from the company of others, she gave herself over to grief and tears. This caused her to become thin and disconsolate, so that she barely resembled the beautiful Giulietta she once had been.

Romeo stayed in touch with her by means of comforting letters in which without fail he gave her reason to hope that they would soon be together. He entreated her to keep her spirits up, to seek distractions and not be so sorrowful because everything would be dealt with in the best way possible. But all was in vain since without Romeo there could be no redress for her suffering.

Giulietta's mother thought that her daughter's unhappiness was caused by the marriage of several of her companions and that she likewise desired a husband. When this thought occurred to her, she communicated it to her husband, saying to him:[29] "Husband, our daughter is leading a wretched life given over entirely to weeping and sighing, and she avoids talking with others as much as she can. Many times have I asked her the cause of her discontent and to this end I have also made extensive enquiries, but I have been unable to learn anything. She always gives me the same answer, that she does not know what is wrong; and all other members of the house shrug their shoulders and do not know what to make of it. There is no doubt that some great passion is tormenting her, since she is visibly wasting away like wax in a flame. And of the thousand possible causes that have occurred to me, only one seems plausible: I strongly suspect that her unhappiness stems from her having seen all her companions become brides this past Carnival, and nobody talks of giving her a husband. She turns eighteen years of age this coming St Euphemia's day,[30] which is why I thought it best to have a word with you. I believe it is now time you sought a good and honourable match for her rather than leaving her unwed, because she is not merchandise to be kept around the house."

After Messer Antonio had heard his wife's words and judged them to the point, he answered her thus: "Wife, since you have not been able to learn anything else about the cause of our daughter's sadness and you think that she should be given a husband, I will make what I deem to be the most fitting negotiations in order to find her a husband suited to our family's social standing. In the meantime, try and find out if perchance she is in love and what husband would be most to her liking." Madonna Giovanna said she would do all she could, and again she did her utmost to find out all she was able to from her daughter and the others in the house; but she learned nothing.

At just this time Count Paris of Lodrone, a very handsome and wealthy young man not yet twenty-five years of age, was introduced to Messer Antonio who, negotiating this match with no little hope of a positive outcome, told his wife of it. As it seemed to her both desirable and very honourable, she told her daughter, whereupon

Giulietta appeared exceedingly distressed and sorrowful. On witnessing this reaction Madonna Giovanna was downcast, not being able to determine what caused it, and after much discussion she said to Giulietta: "Well then, my daughter, judging from what I hear you do not want a husband." "I have absolutely no wish to be married," she answered her mother, adding that if she loved her at all and cared about her, then she was to speak to her no more about a husband.

On hearing her daughter's answer, Giulietta's mother said to her: "What do you want, if not to be married? To become a lay member of a religious order or a nun? Tell me what you want." Giulietta then replied that she had no wish to join a religious order either as a lay person or as a nun, and that she did not know what else she wanted, except to die. Giulietta's answers filled her mother with consternation and sorrow, and she did not know what to say and even less what to do.

All that the other members of the house could say was that after the death of her cousin Giulietta had been very dejected, that she wept incessantly and thereafter was not to be seen at any window. Madonna Giovanna related everything to Messer Antonio, who summoned his daughter and, after a preliminary discussion, said to her: "My daughter, seeing that you are now of marriageable age, I have found you a most noble groom both rich and handsome, who is Lord and Count of Lodrone. Prepare yourself therefore to accept him and to do my bidding, because honourable matches such as these are rarely to be found." With more spirit than becomes a maiden Giulietta boldly replied that she did not wish to marry. Her father was so disturbed that he was close to striking her in anger. He threatened her harshly in sharp terms and ended up by saying that, whether she wanted to or not, within three or four days she was to make up her mind to go to Villafranca with her mother and other women relatives, since Count Paris and his entourage were to go there to see her. She was to offer no objection or resistance to this proposal if she did not want him to beat her to a pulp and make her the most wretched daughter that had ever been born.

Those who have ever experienced the flames of love can imagine Giulietta's thoughts and state of mind. She was so stunned as to appear thunderstruck. After she had recovered she informed Romeo of everything by means of Frate Lorenzo. Romeo wrote back that she should be of good cheer because he would come shortly to take her away from her father's house and bring her to Mantua. Thus she had no choice but to go to Villafranca where her father owned a most beautiful estate. She went there with the same pleasure with which those condemned to death go to the scaffold to be hanged by the neck. Count Paris was there, having already seen her at Mass in church, and although she was thin, pale and despondent, he liked her and came to Verona where he and Messer Antonio concluded the wedding negotiations.

When Giulietta, too, returned to Verona, her father told her that her marriage with Count Paris had been finalised, urging her to rejoice and be of good cheer. Making a great effort of the will, she held back the tears welling up in her eyes and made no reply to her father. With confirmation that wedding preparations were underway for the middle of that coming September and not being able to find any way out of the dire straits in which she found herself, she decided to go in person to talk with Frate Lorenzo and seek his advice on how to get out of the betrothal.

The Feast of the Glorious Assumption of the most blessed Virgin, mother of our Redeemer, was approaching.[31] On this pretext Giulietta sought her mother out and spoke thus to her: "My dear mother, I have no idea what can be causing this terrible sadness that torments me so, for I have been incapable of shaking off my sorrow since Tebaldo died, and I seem to be going progressively from bad to worse, unable to find any remedy. For this reason I thought to attend confession this blessed and holy Feast of the Assumption of our Patron, the Virgin Mary, since perhaps by this means I shall receive some recompense for my tribulations. What do you think, dear mother? Do you think I should act on this plan? If you believe I should follow some other course of action, tell me what it is because I no longer know what to think." Madonna Giovanna, a woman both good and devout, approved of her daughter's intentions, begging her to follow through with her plan and praising her highly for such an idea.

Thus together they went to the Church of St Francis and had Frate Lorenzo summoned. After he had come and entered the confessional, Giulietta took her place on the other side of it and spoke to him thus: "My father, there is nobody in the world who knows better than you what has transpired between my husband and myself, thus there is no need for me to go over it again with you. You will also recall a letter that I sent you to read before you passed it on to my Romeo. In this letter I wrote of how my father had betrothed me to

Count Paris of Lodrone. Romeo wrote back that he would come and take care of things, but God knows when. The fact is that those concerned have arranged that the wedding take place this coming September and that I be made to comply. Since the time is drawing near and I see no way of ridding myself of this Lodrone, who to me seems a thief[32] and murderer, wanting to steal what belongs to others, I have come here for advice and help. I would not want to find myself in jeopardy because of Romeo's written promise to 'come and take care of things', for I am his wife and have consummated the marriage. I cannot belong to anyone but him, and even if I could, I do not wish to, since I intend remaining his and his alone forever. As I now need your help and advice, listen to what I have in mind to do: I would like you, father, to find me trousers, a jacket, and whatever else a youth wears so that thus attired I may slip out of Verona either late in the evening or very early in the morning without anybody recognising me, and I shall go straight to Mantua where I shall take shelter in my Romeo's house."

On hearing this ill-planned scheme which he liked not at all, the worthy friar said: "My daughter, your plan must not be carried out because you would put yourself at too great a risk. You are very young and have had a sheltered upbringing, and you would not be able to withstand the hardship of the journey as you are unused to travelling on foot. Moreover, you do not know the way and would go wandering first this way then that. As soon as your father were to find you not in the house, he would send men out to all the gates of the city and roads beyond, and without a doubt his scouts would easily find you. Once you had been brought back home, your father would insist on knowing why you had left thus dressed as a man, and I do not know how you would endure your family's threats and perhaps the beatings they would give you so as to learn the truth of the matter. Thus where all your efforts had been directed at seeing Romeo, you would lose all hope of ever seeing him again."

Convinced by the friar's sensible words, Giulietta replied: "Since you reject my plan, father, and I accept your reasons for doing so, advise me what to do. Show me how to untangle myself from this mess in which, oh woe! I am at present ensnared so that, as far as possible with less tribulation, I may be reunited with my Romeo, for I cannot live without him. And if you cannot help me in any other way, at least help me not to become somebody else's wife, if I am not to be Romeo's. He has told me that you are skilled at distilling herbs and other things, and that you can prepare a draught which kills those who drink it in two hours, without causing any pain whatsoever. Give me enough of it to free me from the clutches of this thief, since you cannot reunite me with Romeo in any other way. Loving me as I know he does, he would rather I died than ended up alive in someone else's hands. Moreover, you will deliver not only me but my entire family from surpassing shame, because if there is no other way to rescue me from this stormy sea in which I now find myself adrift in a battered boat with no rudder, I give you my solemn word that one night in cold blood I shall slit my throat open with a sharp knife, for I am determined to die rather than be unfaithful to Romeo."

This friar was much given to seeking out new knowledge and had in his day visited many countries and delighted in experimenting and learning about different things. More than anything else he was familiar with the properties of herbs and precious stones, and was one of the greatest distillers of draughts to be found at that time. Amongst other things he used to mix together several sleep-inducing herbs and made them into a paste which he then reduced to a very fine powder of prodigious power. Once it had been drunk with a little water, in less than half an hour it made whoever had drunk it fall into a deep sleep, slowing down all vital functions and so altering the person's appearance that no doctor, however expert and experienced, would pronounce him anything but dead. The person who had drunk the potion then remained in this pleasant death-like state for around forty hours and sometimes more, according to the quantity consumed and the balance of the humours[33] in the consumer's body. Once the powder's effect had worn off, the man or woman awoke exactly as though from a long, sweet sleep, without it causing any further bother or harm.

After he had clearly understood the disconsolate maiden's firm resolve, moved to pity for her he could scarcely hold back his tears. Thus with a voice full of compassion he said: "Come now, my daughter, you must not speak of dying because I assure you that once you die, you will only return here the day of the Last Judgement, when we and our fellow dead will be resurrected. I want you to think about living for as long as God wants. It was he who gave us life, it is he who watches over it for us and, when he sees fit, he reclaims it. So cast aside this gloomy thought. You are young and now you must think of living and enjoying your Romeo. We will find a solution for everything, fear not. As you can see, I have a good name and as a rule I am held in the highest repute by everybody in this magnificent city. If it were known that I had been responsible for your marriage, I would endure great harm and immeasurable loss of reputation. And what would happen if I were to give you poison? I do not have any, and even if I did, I would not give it to you, both because it would mean committing a capital offence against God and also because I would lose my repute in everything. As you can well understand, few usually are the important matters dealt with in which I, given my authority, do not have a hand. Why, less than a fortnight ago the lord of the city called upon my services in dealings of great moment. So, daughter, I shall willingly do all I can for you and Romeo, taking such measures to help you escape that you will remain Romeo's wife and not become Lodrone's, and without you having to die. But we must act in such a way that nobody ever finds out about it. Now you must be resolute and unafraid, and agree to do everything I tell you, for it will not cause you the least harm. Listen to my plan."

Then the friar described his powder in detail to the maiden, telling of its properties and how he had tested it many times and had always found it infallible. "My daughter," said the worthy friar, "this powder of mine is so unique and of such great worth that without causing any harm it will make you sleep for as long as I have specified and if, while you are resting most peacefully, Galen, Hippocrates, Mesuë and Avicenna[34] together with the entire school of illustrious doctors of the past and present were to examine you and feel your pulse, they would all unanimously proclaim you dead. Yet once you have absorbed the powder, you will awaken from that induced sleep as healthy and beautiful as you are when you get out of bed in the morning. Thus by drinking this water as dawn is about to break, you will fall asleep shortly afterwards and on seeing you sleeping when it is time to arise, your family will try unsuccessfully to awaken you. You will have no pulse and will be as cold as ice. Doctors and relatives will be summoned and, in short, everyone will proclaim you dead. Thus towards evening they will have you buried and placed in the Capelletti family tomb where you will spend the night and next day resting comfortably. Then the following night Romeo and I will come to take you out because I shall have sent a messenger to advise him of the matter. Thus he will smuggle you to Mantua where he will keep you in hiding until this blessed peace is made between his people and yours, for I feel that this can be easily achieved. If you do not follow this procedure, I do not know how I can help you with any other. But I repeat: you must be tight-lipped and keep this matter to yourself, or else you will ruin things for yourself and for me."

Giulietta, who would have gone not only into a tomb to find Romeo but into a raging furnace, believed the friar beyond the shadow of a doubt and without thinking twice about it gave her agreement, saying to him: "Father, I will do everything you say, and thus I place myself in your hands. Fear not that I will speak of this matter to anyone, for I shall not breathe a word." The friar immediately hurried to his room and brought the maiden as much powder as would fit in a spoon, wrapped in a little paper. Giulietta took the powder, put it in a bag of hers, and thanked Frate Lorenzo warmly. The friar, who had difficulty in believing that a young girl could have so much self-assurance and courage as to allow herself to be enclosed in a tomb among corpses, said to her: "Tell me, daughter, will you not be afraid of your cousin Tebaldo who was killed only a short time ago and who lies in the tomb where you will be placed, undoubtedly giving off a terrible stench?" "My father," replied the courageous maiden, "you need have no fear of this, for if I believed that I could find Romeo by passing amongst Hell's grievous torments, that eternal fire would not deter me." "Then may it be in the name of our Lord God," said the friar.

Giulietta went back to her mother very happy and on the way home said to her: "Mother, I can tell you for a fact that Frate Lorenzo is a most holy man. He has consoled me to such an extent with his sweet and holy words that he has all but drawn me out of the fearful wretchedness from which I was suffering. He preached such a devout little sermon to me, the most appropriate one imaginable for my malady." Madonna Giovanna, who saw that her daughter was much more cheerful than usual and heard what she was saying, could not hide the happiness that her daughter's joyfulness and comfort gave her, and she replied: "My dear daughter, may God bless you! I am in very good spirits since you are beginning to cheer up, and we are indeed very indebted to this spiritual father of ours. We must hold him dear and help him with our charity since the monastery is poor and every day he prays to God on our behalf. Bear him often in mind and send him some good foodstuff."

Given Giulietta's apparent happiness, Madonna Giovanna believed that she had truly recovered from her former sorrow and she said as much to her husband; both rejoiced and were relieved, and they dismissed their earlier suspicion that she was in love with someone. Although they were unable to imagine the cause of their daughter's unhappiness, they concluded that the death of her cousin or some other singular event had saddened her. Thus they would willingly have refrained from marrying her for another two or three years if it had been possible to do so without loss of honour, because to them she still seemed too young. But arrangements with the Count were already so far advanced that it was impossible to back out of the deal without causing a scandal.

The wedding day was fixed and Giulietta was magnificently arrayed with splendid attire and jewels. She was in good spirits, laughing and jesting, and each hour to her felt more like centuries before the time came to drink the water with the powder dissolved in it. On the eve of the Sunday when she was to be publicly wed, without saying a word to anyone the maiden prepared a glass of water and placed it at the head of the bed without the dame noticing. She slept little if at all that night, turning various thoughts over in her mind. Then as the hour of dawn began to approach when she was to drink the water with the powder in it, she began to imagine Tebaldo as she had seen him, bleeding copiously from the wound in his throat. Thinking that she would be buried next to or perhaps right on top of him, and that in the same burial chamber there were so many dead bodies and bare bones, her body became so cold and her hair stood on end such that, overcome with fear, she trembled like a leaf in the wind. Besides this, an icy sweat spread throughout her limbs as she imagined herself gradually dismembered into a thousand pieces by those dead bodies.

Thus afraid, she remained for a while not knowing what to do. Then having recovered somewhat her courage, she said to herself: "Alas, what am I thinking of doing? Where I am letting myself be put? If by chance I awake before the friar and Romeo arrive, what will happen to me? Scarcely able as I am to bear the slightest unpleasant smell in the house, will I be able to stand the stench surely given off by the decomposing body of Tebaldo? Who knows if in that tomb there are not snakes and thousands of maggots, which I so fear and loathe? And if I do not have the courage to look at them, how will I be able to bear having them all around me and touching me? Then, too, have I not heard over and over again that many dreadful things have taken place at night not only inside tombs but also in churches and cemeteries?"

Led by this fearful thought to imagine countless abhorrent things, Giulietta almost decided not to take the powder and was on the point of spilling it on the floor. Her mind was a jumble of strange thoughts, some prompting her to take the powder, others suggesting to her a thousand and one dangerous eventualities. Finally, after she had been lost in thought for some time and spurred on by her intense and fervent love for Romeo which in her troubles grew, she cast aside her conflicting thoughts and, in a single draught, bravely drank the water with the powder in it after dawn had already begun to cast its rays over the eastern skies. She then began to rest and before long she fell asleep.

Although the dame who slept with Giulietta had realised that all night long her young mistress had slept little if at all, nevertheless she did not notice her drinking the potion and, once out of bed, she set about doing her tasks about the house as she was wont to do. When the time came for the maiden to arise, the dame returned to the bedroom, saying when she got there: "Come on now, it is time to get up!" Having opened the windows and seeing that Giulietta was neither moving nor showing signs of getting up, she approached her and said, shaking her: "Come on now, sleepyhead, up with you!" But it was as if the good dame were talking to the wall. She began to shake her as hard as she could, to pull her nose and prod her, but all in vain. Her vital spirits were so torpid that not even the most dreadful and deafening thunder in the world would have awoken her with the din it makes. Horror-struck by this and seeing that Giulietta gave as much sign of hearing as a dead body would have done, the poor dame was convinced that she was dead. Grief-stricken and sad beyond measure, weeping most bitterly she ran to find Madonna Giovanna to whom she could barely say, gasping and choked with surpassing grief: "My lady, your daughter is dead."

The mother hastened away crying all the while and when she found her daughter reduced to the state already described, there is no need to ask if she was sorrowful and overwhelmed with extreme grief. With her piteous cries cast heavenwards she would have moved stones to pity and quieted tigers at their most fierce after the loss of their young. The weeping and cries of the mother and dame heard all over the house caused everyone to rush to the source of the noise. Giulietta's father hastened there and, after finding his daughter colder than ice and completely senseless, he all but died of grief.

After the event was divulged, gradually the whole city became full of it. Friends and relatives came to the house and the more people there were, the louder the weeping became. The best-known doctors in the city were immediately sent for, who tried all the remedies that they knew to be the most fitting and salutary but without their skills accomplishing any improvement. After they had learned of the sort of life that the maiden had been accustomed to leading for many days, doing nothing but weep and sigh, they were all of the opinion that she had, in fact, died of excessive grief. At this the weeping greatly increased and throughout the whole of Verona everyone lamented such a premature and unexpected death.

But more than anyone else it was the sorrowing mother who wept most bitterly and grieved, refusing all consolation. Embracing her daughter three times, she fainted and appeared as dead as Giulietta, which added to the grief and weeping. There were many women around her who did their best to console her. She had given such free rein to her sorrow and had surrendered herself so completely to its power that, having almost succumbed to despair, she understood nothing of what was said to her and did naught but weep, sigh and send shrieks every now and then up to the heavens, tearing her hair like a mad woman. Messer Antonio was no less sorrowful than she and the less he gave vent to his grief by weeping, the greater it became. Nevertheless, loving his daughter as tenderly as he did, he felt great sorrow but was able to curb it as he was more circumspect.

That morning Frate Lorenzo wrote to Romeo explaining in detail the scheme involving the powder and what had happened. He explained that he would go the following night to remove Giulietta from the tomb and bring her to his room. Romeo thus was to see to coming to Verona in disguise and the friar would wait for him until midnight of the following day when they would do what they thought best. Having written the letter and sealed it, he gave it to a trustworthy friar of his, commanding him to go and find Romeo Montecchi in Mantua that same day and to give the letter to him and nobody else, no matter whom.

The friar set out and arrived in Mantua very early, dismounting at the Convent of St Francis. He first saw to his horse then, while looking for the Father Guardian so as to be given a companion with whom to go about the city doing his business, he found out that one of the friars in that convent had only just died, and because there had been some talk of plague, the health officers decided that without a doubt this was the cause of the said friar's death; the more so since a bubo much larger than an egg was found in his groin, as this was an indisputable and very clear sign of that pestilential illness. At exactly the same time that the friar from Verona was requesting a companion, the health officials arrived and, under threat of very severe punishment by the lord of the city, ordered the Father Guardian not to let anyone whatsoever out of the monastery if he wished to remain in the prince's good graces. The friar who had come from Verona tried to explain that he had only just arrived and had not had contact with anyone; but his efforts were wasted, for he was forced to remain with the other friars in the convent. Hence he did not give that blessed letter to Romeo, nor did he otherwise send word to him. This gave rise to great misfortune and woe, as you will shortly hear.[35]

In the meanwhile, preparations were being made in Verona for the very solemn funeral rites of the maiden that everyone believed dead, and it was decided to perform them late in the evening of that same day. On hearing that Giulietta was dead, Romeo's servant Pietro was stunned and made up his mind to go to Mantua, but first he would wait until it was time to bury the maid and see her taken to the tomb so as to be able to tell his master that he had seen her dead. Provided he was able to leave Verona, he thought to ride by night and enter Mantua as the gate was opened. Thus to the general sorrow of all Verona the coffin with Giulietta in it was taken up late in the afternoon and carried with pomp towards the Church of St Francis accompanied by all the city's priests and friars.

Pietro was so stunned and beside himself with pity for his master, who he knew loved the maiden as he loved no other, that it did not occur to him to go and see Frate Lorenzo and talk with him as he had done at other times; for if he had gone to find the friar, he would have heard the story of the powder, and by telling it to Romeo the subsequent misfortune could have been avoided. Well then, after he had seen Giulietta in the coffin and clearly recognised her, he mounted his horse and having gone at a brisk pace as far as Villafranca, he looked to resting his horse there and sleeping a while. Having arisen then more than two hours before daybreak, he entered Mantua as the sun was rising and went to his master's house.

But let us return to Verona. After the maiden had been borne to the church and the offices for the dead solemnly sung as it is the custom to do in rites such as these, she was placed in the tomb around midnight. The immense marble tomb was outside the church rising above the cemetery and was joined on one side to a wall overlooking an adjacent cemetery where it formed an enclosed space some three or four yards wide. When a corpse was placed in the tomb, the bones of those who had previously been buried in it were thrown into this space, which had narrow openings very high up from the ground. As soon as the tomb was opened, Frate Lorenzo immediately had Tebaldo's body removed to one side; because Tebaldo had been naturally very thin and since dying had lost all his blood, his body had decomposed little and did not smell much. Once the friar had had the burial chamber swept and cleaned, he had the maiden laid out as gently as possible and a pillow placed under her head, since his was the task of having her buried. Following this the burial chamber was locked once more.

When Pietro went into the house he found Romeo still in bed, and once he stood before him he was unable to utter a word, so choked was he by an endless outpouring of sobs and tears. This greatly amazed Romeo who, not imagining what had actually happened but other misfortunes, asked him repeatedly: "Pietro, what is the matter? What news do you bring me from Verona? How are my father and the rest of our people? Speak up, do not keep me in suspense any longer! Whatever can have upset you so much? Come on, out with it!" When Pietro had finally regained control over his grief, in a faint and hesitant voice he told him of Giulietta's death, of how he had seen her carried off for burial, and that she was thought to have died of grief.

On hearing such painful and cruel news, Romeo was almost beside himself for quite some time, then as though out of his mind he leapt out of bed saying: "Ah, Romeo, disloyal and wicked traitor, you most ungrateful of wretches! It is not sorrow that killed your wife, for people do not die of grief. It was you with your cruelty, you were the executioner, you were the murderer. It was you who killed her! She even wrote to you that she would rather die than agree to marry anyone else, and that you were somehow to go and take her away from her father's house. And you, you ungrateful, lazy, half-hearted wretch, you cur, you promised her faithfully that you would go, that you would do something, you urged her not to lose heart, while you dillydallied from one day to the next, irresolute about what she wanted you to do. So you twiddled your thumbs and Giulietta is dead. Giulietta is dead and you are alive? Ah, traitor! How many times did you tell her in writing and to her face that you could not live without her? And yet you are still alive! Where do you think she is? She is wandering around in here, waiting for you to follow her and saying to herself: 'Behold the liar! Behold the deceitful lover and faithless husband who on hearing that I am dead can bear to go on living!' Forgive me, forgive me, my most beloved wife, for I confess my very grave sin. But since the boundless, overwhelming sorrow that I feel is not enough to take my life, I myself will perform what ought to be sorrow's task. I shall take my own life, in defiance of sorrow and death who do not want to do it for me."

Thus speaking he took up the sword that was at the head of the bed and having drawn it straight away from its sheath he turned it towards his chest, pointing it at his heart. But his good servant Pietro reacted so promptly that he was unable to wound himself, and in a trice he took the sword from Romeo's hand. He then spoke to him as all faithful servants should speak to their masters in similar circumstances, and wisely reprimanding him for such madness he comforted him as best he knew how, begging him to go on living since nothing could be done in this world to help the dead woman.

That most cruel news of such an unexpected event had so deeply stunned Romeo that it was as if he had turned to stone or marble. No tears could escape his eyes and anyone looking at his face would have said that he was more like a statue than a man. But it was not long before his tears began to flow so abundantly as to appear a lively fountain pouring out spring water. Even the most hardened of barbarian hearts would have been moved to pity by the words he uttered while weeping and sighing. Then as his inner grief began to pour out, so Romeo, his mind in confusion, began to give way to his bitter passions and black, desperate thoughts; and since his dear Giulietta was dead, he decided that under no circumstances did he want to go on living. But he gave no outward sign of his drastic resolve, nor did he say anything. Rather he kept his intentions to himself so that when the time came neither his servant nor anybody else would prevent him from carrying out what he had decided to do.

Thus he ordered Pietro, who was the only other person in the room, not to mention his wife's death to anyone and even less was he to disclose the mistake of wanting to kill himself in which he had almost fallen. He then told him to make ready two fresh horses because he wanted the two of them to go to Verona. "I want you," he said, "to set out shortly without saying a word to anyone. Once you are in Verona, do not mention to my father that I am about to arrive, but see to finding the tools necessary for opening the tomb where my wife is buried and some props to keep it open, because I shall enter Verona late this evening. I shall go straight to the cottage you have behind our orchard and between three and four o'clock we will go to the cemetery because I wish to see my ill-fated wife once more, lying there dead. Then early the next morning I shall leave Verona unrecognised with you following close behind me and we will return here." Not long after he sent Pietro back.

After Pietro had left, Romeo wrote his father a letter asking his forgiveness for having married without his permission and telling him all about his love and how his marriage had come about. He then begged him in the most affectionate terms to organise for a solemn office for the dead to be celebrated at Giulietta's burial place, as she was his daughter-in-law; he was to see to it that this office be repeated indefinitely by providing a bequest from his revenue. As Romeo had inherited some property from an aunt of his who had named Romeo her sole heir on dying, he also made provision for Pietro to live comfortably without having to depend on others. He entreated his father to take care of these two matters, declaring these to be his last wishes. And since his aunt had died only a few days earlier, he begged his father to have the first profits from his inherited estates distributed to the poor for the love of God. Having written and sealed the letter, he concealed it close to his chest. He then took a small phial filled with deadly poison and, dressed as a German, he mounted his horse, giving those left in the house to believe that he would return early the next day. Nobody was to go with him.

Thus by travelling steadily he entered Verona at eventide and went straight to look for Pietro whom he found at home and who had made all the arrangements asked of him. Thus about the fourth hour after sunset they headed from there towards the Citadel, taking with them such instruments and tools as they deemed necessary and they arrived at the Church of St Francis cemetery without encountering any obstacles. Having found there the tomb in which Giulietta was lying, they opened it deftly with their implements then propped the cover open with stable supports. On Romeo's orders Pietro had brought with him a small lantern known variously as a "blind" or "deaf" lantern[36] which, when uncovered, assisted them in opening the tomb and placing the supports carefully. Romeo went inside and saw his beloved wife who indeed appeared dead. He immediately fell completely senseless by Giulietta's side, more dead than she was, and he remained unconscious for some time, so overcome with grief that he came close to dying. Having then regained consciousness he embraced his beloved wife and kissing her repeatedly, he bathed her pale face with burning tears, his bitter weeping preventing him from uttering a single word.

After weeping at length, he gave voice to a flood of words that would have moved the most hardened hearts in the world to pity. Having decided at last that he no longer wished to live, he took out the small phial that he had brought, emptied the poisoned water that it contained into his mouth, and swallowed it in a single draught. Once he had done this, he called Pietro who was waiting in a corner of the cemetery and told him to come up onto the tomb. When he had done so and was leaning at the edge of the tomb, Romeo spoke to him thus: "Here you see, oh, Pietro! my wife. You already know something of the love which I bore her and still bear her. I am well aware that I could as much live without her as a body can live without a soul, thus I brought with me the envenomed water[37] which, as you know, kills a man in less than an hour. I drank it gladly and willingly in order to die here next to the woman I so loved in life. This I do so that I may at least be buried with her once I am dead if I am not permitted to be with her while I am alive. You can see the phial wherein was the water which, if you remember, we were given in Mantua by that man from Spoleto who kept asps and other serpents. May God in his mercy and infinite goodness forgive me, for I have not killed myself to offend him but so as not to remain alive without my dear wife. And if you see my eyes wet with tears, do not think that I am weeping out of self-pity because I am dying so young; rather my weeping is caused by the profound grief that I feel for the death of her who was worthy of living a more happy and peaceful life. You are to give this letter to my father to whom I have written telling him what I want him to do after my death regarding both this tomb and my servants in Mantua. I have seen to it that you, who have served me faithfully, will have no need to go on serving others. I am certain that my father will carry out all that I ask of him in my letter. Off with you now! I can feel death close at hand because I am aware that the poison in the deadly water is already paralysing my limbs. Close up the tomb and let me die next to my wife."

Pietro was so grief-stricken by what Romeo had said that he thought his heart would break within him from the boundless sorrow that he felt. His outpouring of words to his master was wasted for no longer could anything counteract the poisonous water which had by this time spread throughout his entire body. Having taken Giulietta in his arms and kissing her constantly, Romeo awaited his unavoidable end, now close at hand, all the while telling Pietro to close the tomb.

Giulietta, in whom the powder had already run its course, awoke precisely at that time. Feeling herself kissed, she suspected that it was the friar who, after coming to take her from the tomb to his room, was holding her in his arms and, spurred on by lust, was kissing her. She said: "Ah, Father Lorenzo, is this the trust that Romeo had in you? Move away!" And rousing herself to escape from his arms, she opened her eyes and saw she was in Romeo's arms, for she recognised him easily even though he was dressed as a German. "Alas, you are here, my life?" she said, "Where is Frate Lorenzo? Why do you not take me out of this tomb? Let us away, for the love of God!"

When Romeo saw Giulietta open her eyes and heard her speak, thereby realising that she was not dead but alive, he was overwhelmed simultaneously with happiness and grief of unbelievable and incalculable magnitude. Weeping and holding his beloved wife tightly against his chest, he said: "Ah, life of my life and heart of my body, what man alive ever felt as much joy as I do at this moment? I was convinced that you were dead and now I am holding you in my arms, alive and well! But what suffering ever equalled mine, what most heartfelt sorrow compares to my grief, since I feel that I have reached the end of my wretched days and my life is fading when more than ever it behooves me to live! For if I go on living another half-hour, this is all the time I have left in this life. What one person ever experienced simultaneously more extreme happiness and boundless grief than I clearly feel? I am more happy than words can describe, overflowing with joy and contentment, since I suddenly see you alive, my sweet wife, whom I believed dead and for whom I have wept so bitterly. Truly, my most loving wife, it is only right that in this case I rejoice with you. Yet I suffer incalculable grief and sorrow without equal when I think that very soon I shall be allowed no longer to see, hear and remain with you, enjoying your most sweet company that I so longed for. It is indeed true that the joy of seeing you alive greatly exceeds the grief besetting me as the time draws near when I must leave you. And I pray the Lord our God that the years by which he is shortening my unhappy youth, he add to yours.

May he grant you a long life and a happier destiny than mine, for I feel that my life is already coming to an end."

Giulietta, who had already raised herself up somewhat, said to Romeo on hearing what he was saying: "What is the meaning of these words, my lord, that you are now uttering? Is this the comfort you wish to give me? Have you come here from Mantua to give me news of this kind? What is the matter with you?" The unfortunate Romeo then told her about the poison he had drunk. "Alas! Alas!" said Giulietta. "What is this I hear? What are you telling me? Woe is me! From what I hear then, Frate Lorenzo did not write to you about the plan that he and I had devised together. And yet he promised me he would write telling you everything!" Thus overwhelmed with the most bitter grief, weeping, crying out, sighing and becoming almost beside herself with anguish, she related in detail what she and the friar had planned so that she would not be compelled to wed the husband her father wished her to have.

When Romeo heard this, sorrow infinitely increased his woes. While Giulietta was wildly bewailing their misfortune and invoking heaven and the stars together with all the most merciless elements, Romeo saw there the body of Tebaldo whom he had killed in the fight several months earlier, as you have already heard. Having recognised him, he turned towards him and said: "Tebaldo, wherever you may be, you must know that I was not trying to harm you but rather I entered the fray to check it, and I advised you to make your men withdraw because I would make mine lay down their arms. But full as you were of fury and age-old hatred, you did not heed my words; instead you fell upon me with a treacherous heart in order to harm me. Forced as I was by you and having lost my patience, I refused to fall back so much as an inch and as I defended myself your ill-luck so had it that I killed you. I now ask your forgiveness for the offence I did you, the more so since I had already become your relative by taking your cousin as my wife. If you desire revenge from me, you have obtained it. And what greater revenge could you wish for than knowing that he who killed you should have poisoned himself in your presence and is voluntarily dying in front of you, to end up buried next to you? If in life we waged war, in death we will have no quarrel within our shared tomb."

On hearing the husband's piteous talk and his wife's weeping, Pietro was dumbstruck, not knowing if what he was seeing and hearing was true or if in fact he was dreaming; nor did he know what to say or do, so stunned was he. Wretched Giulietta, the most sorrowful of women since her sorrow knew no end, addressed Romeo: "Since it did not please God that we live together, may it at least please him that I be buried here with you. But come now what may, you can be sure that I will never leave here without you." After taking her again in his arms, Romeo began to plead lovingly with her to take heart and to think about living, because he would depart comforted by the certainty that she was still alive; and he dwelt at some length on this matter. He felt himself gradually losing consciousness, his vision was almost completely blurred and he was so lacking in physical strength that he could no longer sit up. Thus giving way he collapsed, and looking his wife pitifully in the face, said: "Alas, my life, I am dying."

For whatever reason, Frate Lorenzo had not wished to take Giulietta to his room the night she was buried. Seeing that Romeo did not turn up, the following night accompanied by a trusted friar of his he then went armed with tools to open the tomb, arriving just as Romeo collapsed. Noticing the open tomb and recognising Pietro, he said: "Good health to you! Where is Romeo?" Hearing the friar's voice and recognising him, Giulietta said raising her head: "May God forgive you! You did a fine job of sending the letter to Romeo!" "I did send it," replied the friar, "Friar Anselmo, whom you know, took it. Why do you say this?" Weeping bitterly, Giulietta answered: "Come on up and you will see." The friar climbed up and seeing Romeo lying almost lifeless, said: "Romeo, my son, what is the matter?" Romeo opened his weary eyes, recognised him and said softly that he entrusted Giulietta to him, that he no longer needed either help or counsel, and that, having repented his sins, he asked for God's and the friar's forgiveness for them. The ill-fated lover was barely able to utter these last words and lightly beat his breast before his strength drained away and, after closing his eyes, he died.

I do not have the heart to show how grievous, agonizing and almost unbearable this was to his disconsolate wife, but let those who love truly, imagine how it would be to find themselves part of such a horrible spectacle. Lamenting wretchedly and to no purpose, she wept for him at length; then calling his beloved name over and over in vain, overcome with anguish she fell unconscious over her husband's body and remained senseless for some time. The friar and Pietro, both extremely grief-stricken, managed to revive her, whereupon she wrung her hands and weeping without restraint, she shed as many tears as any woman ever did.

Giulietta then said, kissing the dead body: "Ah, sweetest haven of all my thoughts and of all the pleasure I have ever known, my beloved and only lord, how bitter now has your sweetness become to me![38] You have run your course while you are still in the bloom of your lovely and fair youth, for you did not cherish life which is so highly valued by everyone else. You chose to die when others most delight in living, and you have arrived at the destination which everybody must reach sooner or later. My lord, you came to finish your days in the lap of the woman whom you loved above all else and by whom you are loved as by no other, and you have come to bury yourself of your own free will there where you believed her to be dead and buried. Never did you think that I would weep these most bitter and heart-felt tears for you. Never would you have believed that you would not find me on going to the other world. I am convinced that on not finding me there you returned here to see if I am following you. Do I not sense that your spirit, wandering around in here, is leaving and is already amazed, or rather, is grieved that I should be delaying so? My lord, I can see you, I can hear you, I recognise you and know that the only thing you are waiting for is for me to come with you. Do not fear, my lord, doubt not that I wish to remain here without your company, for life without you would be much more arduous and more agonizing still than any imaginable way of dying, because without you I would not be alive, and even if it seemed to others that I was, living thus for me would be like a slow and painful death. Thus can you be assured, my dear lord, that very soon I shall come and be with you for ever. And in what company more trusted and dear to me can I depart this wretched life of suffering, than by coming after you and following in your footsteps? Absolutely none, as far as I believe."

Close at hand and overcome with boundless pity, the friar and Pietro were weeping as they did their utmost to comfort her, but all in vain. Frate Lorenzo said to her: "My daughter, what is done cannot be undone. If Romeo could be brought back to life with tears, we would all dissolve into tears to help him; but nothing can be done. Take comfort and think about living, and if you do not wish to return home, I shall see to putting you in a very devout convent where you will be able to pray for the soul of your Romeo while serving God." She adamantly refused to listen to him, but persevering in her dire resolve, she lamented not being able to restore Romeo's life by offering her own, and she determined to die. Having then drawn her spirits[39] together within herself, without uttering a word she died with Romeo in her lap.

While the two friars and Pietro were busying themselves around the dead maiden believing she had fainted, the *podestà's*[40] men saw the light in the tomb as they happened by there and ran up. Once they arrived, they took hold of the friars and Pietro, and having heard the pitiful fate of the star-crossed lovers, they left the friars well guarded and led Pietro to Lord Bartolomeo, explaining to him how they had found him. After dawn had already broken, Lord Bartolomeo arose and insisted on seeing the two bodies, having had the entire story of the two lovers told to him in detail.

Word of this event spread throughout all Verona with the result that young and old came running. The friars and Pietro were forgiven and, to the general sorrow of the whole city and the particular sorrow of the Montecchi and Capelletti, the funeral rites were carried out with great pomp. The lord of the city ordered that the lovers remained buried in that same tomb, which was why peace was made between the Montecchi and Capelletti, although it did not last long. After Romeo's father had read his son's letter and grieved keenly, he carried out his wishes in full. The following epitaph was engraved over the tomb of the two lovers; it reads:

Romeo believed that his fair bride
was already dead and as he no longer wished to live,
he took his life at her bosom
with what is called "serpent" water.
When she learned of the cruel event
she turned weeping to her lord
and fully vented her grief over him,
calling heaven and the stars unjust.
Seeing his life, alas!, come to an end,
more dead than he she could barely utter: "Oh, God,
grant that I may follow my lord:
this alone I beg and seek, this alone I desire,
that wherever he may go, I go with him."
And thus saying she then died of grief.

# *Pierre Boaistuau*

Histoire troisiesme, "De deux amans, dont l'un mourut de venin, l'autre de tristesse."

*(Histoires tragiques,* novella 3)

## *SUMMARY OF THE THIRD TALE* [41]

I am certain that those who measure the greatness of God's works according to the capability of their crude understanding will not readily believe this tale, as much for the variety of strange happenings described therein as for the novelty of such a rare and perfect love. Thus it is that I can assert once and for all that I will not include in this work any fable which I could not confirm by consulting annals and chronicles, or which does not meet with the general approval of those who have seen it, or which is not authorised by some famous Italian or Latin historian. Those who have read in Pliny, Valerius, Plutarch[42] and several other authors that in former times there were numerous men and women who died from excessive joy, will not doubt that it is possible to die from the furious flames of an overly ardent love. If this love takes hold of a receptive subject and does not encounter strong resistance to serve as protection in impeding the violence of its course, it gradually undermines and destroys so thoroughly the natural faculties that the spirit, completely surrendering, departs this life. This is borne out by the piteous and unfortunate death of two lovers who uttered their last sighs in one and the same tomb in Verona, where their bones still rest to this day, to the great amazement of all: a tale no less astounding than true.

## *THIRD TALE*

### *Of two lovers, one of whom died of poison, the other of unhappiness*[43]

If the particular attachment that people rightly have for their birthplace does not deceive you, I believe that you will agree with me that few are the cities in Italy which can surpass Verona, as much for the navigable river, the Adige, which flows almost through the middle of the city and by means of which much trading with Germany is carried out, as likewise for the appearance of the fertile mountains and delightful valleys which surround it, with their numerous crystal clear, gushing springs used for local convenience. I shall refrain from describing in detail several other singular features such as the four bridges and countless other venerable monuments to the past that reveal themselves from day to day to those who are curious to behold them. This is what I wished to investigate going back a little further, more especially as the true tale that I hereafter wish to relate depends on it. So recent still is the memory of this tale nowadays in Verona that the eyes of those who witnessed that piteous spectacle have barely dried.

When Della Scala[44] was lord of Verona, there were two families in the city renowned above all others as much for their wealth as for their nobility. Montesche was the name of one of the families, the other, Capellet. But as there is more often than not envy amongst those of equally high standing, a feud sprang up between them as well and although the original cause of this feud was slight and of no consequence, with time it flared up to such an extent that in the various plots that were undertaken on both sides, several people lost their lives. Bartolomeo della Scala (of whom we have already spoken), being lord of the city and seeing such unrest in his principality, strove by all possible means to subdue and reconcile these two houses, but completely in vain for their hatred was so deeply rooted that it could not be tempered by common sense or counsel. Thus his only achievement was to make them lay down their arms temporarily while he awaited a more opportune time when he hoped to settle everything else at greater leisure.

While things were at this pass, one of the Montesches, Rhomeo by name, not yet twenty-one years of age and the most handsome and best endowed nobleman amongst all of Verona's youth, fell in love with a young Veronese lady, and in a few days he was so captivated by her charming ways that he abandoned all other pursuits in order to serve and honour her. After several letters, messages, and gifts, he at last made up his mind to speak to her, broaching to her the matter of his passion. This he did without achieving anything, for she, raised as she had been in the ways of virtue, replied so unequivocally cutting short his advances that he could have no occasion in the future to persist any further; and so stern was she that she did not even grace him with a single glance. But the more intractable the youth saw she was, the more enflamed he became.

After having persevered for several months in this servitude without finding any cure for his passion, he resolved at last to leave Verona to see if a change of setting would bring about a change of heart in him. He said to himself: "What good does it do me to love an ungrateful woman, since she scorns me in this way? I follow her everywhere, and she flees me. I cannot live unless I am near her, yet her only happiness is when she is not in my company. Therefore from now on I want to flee her presence, for perhaps if I behold her no more this fire of mine, which is fed by her beautiful eyes, will gradually go out." But while he was thinking about carrying these thoughts out, immediately his resolve changed so that, not knowing what to do, he spent his days and nights complaining and lamenting wondrously, for love beckoned him from so close at hand and had imprinted the young lady's beauty so firmly in his heart that, being incapable of resisting it any more, he completely surrendered and gradually wasted away like snow in the sun.

His relatives and friends were amazed by this and greatly lamented his misfortune; but more than all others a companion of his, older and wiser than Rhomeo, began to reprimand him bitterly, for the friendship which he bore him was so great that he, too, felt his torment and shared his passion. This was why, on seeing him disturbed sometimes by his amorous flights of fancy, he said to him: "Rhomeo, I am greatly amazed at how you waste your best years in this way pursuing someone who scorns and dismisses you without having any consideration either for your lavish expenditure, for your honour, for your tears, or even for your wretched life, which moves the most steadfast to pity. For this reason I beg you, in the name of our long friendship and of your own health, that in the future you learn to be your own master, without renouncing your freedom to one so ungrateful. From what I can gather from what has happened between you and her, either she is in love with someone else, or she has resolved never to love anyone. You are young, well endowed with Fortune's gifts, the most handsome nobleman in this city; you are well educated and an only child. What heartache for your poor old father and your other relatives to see you thus plunged in this abyss of vices, and at an age when you ought to be giving them some expectation of your future achievements. From now on, then, begin to recognise the folly in which you have lived up until now. Cast from your eyes love's blindfold which prevents you from following the righteous path trodden by your ancestors. Or if you feel yourself such a slave to your desires, direct your affections elsewhere and choose a mistress worthy of them; henceforth do not sow your woes in such poor soil that you reap no fruit from it. The time of year is approaching when there will be gatherings of women throughout the city at which you will be able to look so favourably on someone that she will make you forget your previous loves."

The youth, carefully listening to all his friend's convincing arguments, began to temper his ardour somewhat and to realise that all his friend's admonishments were well-intentioned. He decided from then on to put them into effect, attending at random all the banquets and gatherings in the city without favouring any one woman over the others. He went on behaving like this for two or three months, thinking in this way to extinguish the sparks of his former flame. It happened then several days later, around the time of the Christmas festivities, that people began organising masked banquets, according to custom. Since Anthoine Capellet[45] was head of his family and one of the foremost lords in the city, he held a banquet and, to enhance its importance, he invited all Verona's nobility, men and women alike, which included as well the majority of the city's young people.

The Capellet family (as we have pointed out at the beginning of this tale)[46] was on bad terms with the Montesches, which was why the latter were not at the banquet, with the exception of the young Rhomeo Montesche who arrived masked after supper, accompanied by several other young noblemen. After they had remained for some time with their faces covered by their masks, they removed them. Somewhat uncomfortable, Rhomeo withdrew to a corner of the hall, but because of the brightness of the torches that had been lit, he was immediately noticed by everyone, especially the women, for besides the innate beauty with which nature had endowed him, they admired even more his confidence and the fact of his having dared to enter with such familiarity the house of those who had little reason to wish him well. Nevertheless the Capellets, hiding their hatred either out of consideration for those present or respect for his age, harmed him neither with deeds nor words. For this reason he was able to gaze openly and at leisure on the women, which he managed to do with such good grace that there was no woman who did not derive pleasure from his presence.

After he had passed judgement on the excellence of each woman in turn according as fancy led him, he espied amongst the others one extremely beautiful young girl who, although he had never seen her before, appealed to him more than all others. To her he gave pride of place in his heart for unsurpassable beauty. While he was regaling her ceaselessly with piteous looks, the love which he used to bear his first young lady was vanquished by this new fire, which then grew and strengthened to such an extent that death alone could ever extinguish it, as you will understand from one of the most unusual tales that mortal man could imagine.

Thus feeling himself buffeted by this new storm, the young Rhomeo did not know how to react; but so dumbfounded and shaken was he by these new flames that he almost did not know himself, with the result that he lacked the boldness to enquire who she was, devoting all his attention to feasting his eyes on the sight of her, and by this means he admitted love's sweet poison, by which he was at last so affected that a cruel death brought his days to an end. The woman for whom Rhomeo suffered such an unusual passion was named Julliette and was the daughter of Capellet, master of the house in which this gathering was being held. As her eyes wandered here and there, she noticed by chance Rhomeo who seemed to her the most handsome nobleman she had ever looked upon freely. Then love, which was lying in ambush and had never before besieged the tender heart of this young maid, touched her so deeply that whatever resistance she was able to make, she was powerless to resist its strength. From that moment she began to scorn all the splendours of the party and felt no pleasure in her heart except when she had cast a furtive glance at Rhomeo or received one from him. After they had satisfied their impassioned hearts with countless loving looks which more often than not met and became one, the burning rays issuing from them were ample witness to the beginning of their love.

Once love had made this breach in the lovers' hearts, just as they were both seeking some way of talking to one another, Fortune offered them a ready occasion, for a gentleman from the gathering took Julliette by the hand to have her take part in the dance of the torch,[47] which she was able to perform so well and with such grace that for that day it was she who won the prize of honour out of all the young girls in Verona. Rhomeo, having foreseen the place where she would withdraw from the dance, came forward and conducted matters so judiciously that on his way back he was able to be beside her. At the end of the dance Julliette returned to the same spot where she had been at the beginning and ended up seated between Rhomeo and another youth called Marcucio,[48] a courtier much loved by everyone who, because of his witticisms and fine ways was warmly received at all gatherings. Marcucio, as bold amongst virgins as a lion is amongst lambs, seized Julliette's hand forthwith. In winter and summer alike he habitually had hands as cold as a piece of mountain ice, even when he was near the fire. Rhomeo, who was on Julliette's left, seeing that Marcucio was holding her right hand, took Julliette's other hand so as not to fail in his duty and, clasping it tightly for a while, felt so overwhelmed by this new favour that he was dumbstruck, incapable of replying. But Julliette, who realised from the change in his colour that this shortcoming was due to uncontrollable love, turned towards him eager to hear him speak. In a voice trembling with both virginal shyness and modesty, she said to him: "Blessed be the moment of your arrival at my side"; then, though intending to go on, love so sealed her lips that she was unable to finish what she had started out to say.

At this the youth, beside himself with joy and gladness, asked her with a sigh the reason for this fortunate blessing. A little more self-assured, Julliette answered him, smiling and glancing compassionately at him: "My lord, be not amazed if I bless your coming, because for a long time Lord Marcucio's icy hand has completely frozen my own, and you have warmed it for me with your charm." To this Rhomeo promptly replied: "My lady, if heaven has so favoured me that I have done you some agreeable service by turning up here by chance, I deem it put to good use, wishing as I do for no greater good to crown all the joys that I ask in this world than to serve, obey, and honour you wherever my life may lead me, as you will see beyond all doubt whenever it pleases you to put it to the test. Moreover, if you derived some warmth from the touch of my hand, well may I assure you that flames are dead compared with the bright sparks and blazing fire issuing from your beautiful eyes. So thoroughly has this fire taken hold of all my senses that, if you do not favour me by sending your heavenly graces to my assistance, I await only the moment when I shall be wholly consumed and reduced to ashes."

Scarcely had he finished these last words than the game of the torch came to an end, so Julliette, all aflame with love, clasping his hand tightly, was unable to make any other reply than to whisper to him: "My dear friend, I know not what more certain evidence you want of my love save my assurance that I belong no less to you than you do to yourself, being as I am ready and willing to obey you in all things honourable. I beg that you be content with this for the present and that you await some other more favourable occasion when we will be able to speak more privately of our affairs." Hearing his friends urging him to leave and not knowing how he could see again her who held his life and death in her hands, Rhomeo took it upon himself to ask a friend who she was. His friend replied that she was the daughter of Capellet, master of the house in which the banquet had just taken place. Indignant beyond measure that Fortune had directed him to such a dangerous place, Rhomeo deemed that it was all but impossible to bring his undertaking to an end.

For her part Julliette, eager to know who the young man was who had flattered her so courteously that evening causing the new wound she how felt in her heart, called an aged lady-in-waiting on whose milk she had been suckled and raised and said to her, leaning forward: "Mother, who are those two youths going out first with two torches in front of them?" To this the dame replied by indicating their family allegiances. Then she questioned her again: "Who is that youth holding a mask and wearing a damask cloak?" "That is Rhomeo Montesche, son of the capital enemy of your father and his allies," she replied. But just the mention of the name Montesche left the maiden completely confused and in deep despair of ever being able to have her beloved Rhomeo as her husband, given the long-standing feud between her family and his. She was nonetheless able (for the time being) to hide her worry and disappointment so well that the dame was not aware of it, but urged her to retire to her room to lie down. Julliette obeyed, but while she was lying in bed and trying to rest as usual, a great storm of confused thoughts began to engulf and buffet her in such a way that she could not even close her eyes. As she tossed this way and that, many fantastic thoughts ran through her mind, making her first resolve to abandon this love affair completely, then to go ahead with it.

Thus the maiden was troubled by two contradictory thoughts, one of which directed her to pursue her resolve while the other laid before her the grave danger towards which she was unwisely rushing. After having wandered at length in love's labyrinth, she was no closer to making up her mind but cried incessantly and reproached herself, saying: "Ah, wretched and unfortunate creature that I am! What causes this unfamiliar tribulation in my soul, which allows me no respite? Woe is me! How do I know if this youth loves me as he says? Could it be that under the cloak of his honeyed words he wants to deprive me of my honour in order to take revenge on my relatives, who have offended his? Would he thus make me the talking piece of all Verona because of my everlasting shame?" Then straight afterwards she dismissed her initial suspicions, saying: "How could it ever be possible that disloyalty and betrayal lurk beneath such beauty and unmatched sweetness? If it is true that the face faithfully conveys our thoughts, I can be sure that he loves me, for I have seen him change colour so often when he was talking to me, so carried away and beside himself that I ought not wish for any other surer sign of this love of his which I hope will accompany me right up to the last breath I take; providing he marries me, that is, for perhaps this new alliance will bring about lasting peace and love between his family and mine." With this fixed thought in mind, her expression changed to joy whenever she noticed Rhomeo pass by her door, and she watched him out of the corner of her eye until she lost sight of him.

After having carried on like this for several days Rhomeo, not being content with just looking, studied daily the situation of the house. One particular day he noticed Julliette at the window of her room which looked out on a very narrow street on the opposite side of which there was a garden. This led Rhomeo (who feared that their love might be revealed) to refrain henceforth from passing by her door during the day; but as soon as night with its dark mantle had covered the earth, alone and armed he would turn up in this alley. After he had been there several times in vain Julliette, impatient in her lovesickness, stood one evening at her window and because of the moonlight she easily noticed her Rhomeo close by her window, as long awaited by her as she was by him. She then said to him very quietly, with a tear in her eye and sighs punctuating her words: "Lord

Rhomeo, you appear to me too rash by far with your life, exposing it at such an hour to the mercy of those who have so little occasion to wish you well. If they had caught you there by surprise, they would have cut you to pieces; in addition my honour, dearer to me than my life, would be for ever compromised." "My lady," Rhomeo replied, "my life is in the hands of God, who alone can dispose of it. Thus if someone sought to take my life, I would show him in your presence that I am able to defend it; however, I do not hold it so dear nor in such esteem that I would not sacrifice it for you if necessary. And should I be so unfortunate as to be deprived here of my life, I would have no cause to regret it except that in losing it I would lose the means with which to show you the love and servitude I bear you; nor do I wish to preserve it for any pleasure it may afford me, nor for any other reason apart from loving, serving, and honouring you until the last breath I take."

As soon as he had finished what he had to say, love and pity then began to take hold of Julliette's heart and, resting her head on her hand and with her face bathed in tears, she answered Rhomeo: "Lord Rhomeo, I beg that you speak to me no more of these things, for the dread alone aroused in me by such a misfortune is enough to make me hover between life and death, so bound is my heart to yours that I would feel in equal measure the slightest possible disturbance that could befall you as though it were my own. Moreover, if you desire your own and my welfare, I beg that you let me know in few words what your plans for the future are, for if you are aspiring to liberties other than those which my honour allows, you are making a great mistake. But if your intentions are pure, if the love which you claim to bear me is based on virtue, and if marriage crowns it, on taking me as your lawfully wedded wife you will become so much a part of me that, disregarding both the obedience and respect which I owe my parents and the long-standing enmity between your family and mine, I shall make you master and eternal lord of myself and all I possess; and I shall be ready and willing to follow you wherever you so order me. But if you have some other intention, if you think to gather the fruit of my virginity under the pretext of some wanton love, you are making a grave mistake and I beg you to cease and leave me to live from now on in peace with my kind."

Rhomeo, who aspired to nothing else, raising his clasped hands to heaven replied, overjoyed and happy beyond belief: "My lady, since it so pleases you to do me the honour of accepting me as your husband, I agree and consent to it from the bottom of my heart, which you will have as a pledge and sure proof of what I say until God grants that I show it to you with deeds. And in order that I may set matters in motion, tomorrow I shall go and seek the counsel of Friar Laurens who, besides being my spiritual father, is in the habit of directing me in all my other private affairs. If it so pleases you, meet me again without fail at the same time and place so that I may let you know what I have arranged with him." This she willingly granted, and their conversation came to an end without Rhomeo having received any other favour from her that evening apart from spoken ones.

Friar Laurens (who will be dealt with more fully later on) was an aged Doctor of Theology of the Order of the Friars Minor who, besides the successful profession that he had made of holy letters, was wondrously versed in Philosophy and a great investigator of the secrets of nature, famed even for having knowledge of Magic and of other hidden and occult sciences. This to no extent detracted from his reputation, for he did not abuse his knowledge at all. This friar had so completely won the hearts of the citizens of Verona with his integrity and goodness that he heard the confession of almost all of them; and there was no one, young or old, who did not revere and love him; because of his great discretion, he was even summoned as often as not to take part in the most private dealings of the city's lords. Amongst those that greatly favoured him were Della Scala, lord of Verona, every last member of the Montesche and the Capellet families, and several others.

The young Rhomeo (as we have already said) had always had from a very tender age I know not what particular friendship with Friar Laurens and told him all his secrets. This is why Rhomeo, after leaving Julliette, went straight to the Church of St Francis where he went over the entire story of his love with the friar, including the decision he and Julliette had taken to marry; he ended by saying that he would rather die dishonourably than not keep his promise to her. In reply the good man begged him to take his time and think it over, after having admonished him somewhat and made him aware of all the disadvantages of this clandestine marriage; yet he was unable to bend him. Thus won over by his determination and foreseeing as well that this marriage would perhaps be the means by which these two family lines were reconciled, he at last granted Rhomeo's request, on the condition that he be given a day's grace to work out how he could help them.

But if for his part Rhomeo was anxious to put his affairs in order, for her part Julliette likewise carried out her duty well, for seeing that she had nobody close to her in whom she could confide her passion, she took it into her head to impart everything to her wet-nurse who slept in the same room as she did and who acted as her lady-in-waiting; to her she entrusted in full the secret of the love between herself and Rhomeo. Although the dame was at first reluctant to comply, Julliette at last succeeded so well in convincing her and winning her over that she promised to obey Julliette in whatever she could. Thus she sent her off with all possible haste to go and talk to Rhomeo so as to find out from him how they could marry; and he was to let her know what had been decided between himself and Friar Laurens.

Rhomeo told the dame that he had informed Friar Laurens of his affairs the day before, that the friar had put things off until the following day, which was that very day, and that he had returned from speaking with him for the second time barely an hour earlier. He further explained how he and Friar Laurens had decided that the following Saturday Julliette was to ask leave of her mother to attend confession; she was to be in a certain chapel of the Church of St Francis, where the friar would secretly marry them; she was to be there without fail. Such was Julliette's skill and discretion in doing this that her mother granted her request and accompanied only by the good dame and a young woman, she went there on the appointed day. No sooner had she entered the church than she had the learned Friar Laurens summoned; she was told that he was in the confessional and that he would be informed of her arrival.

As soon as Friar Laurens learned of Julliette's arrival, he went into the main part of the church and told the dame and the young woman to go and attend Mass, adding that he would have them summoned when he had finished with Julliette. Once she had entered the cell with Friar Laurens, he closed the door behind them, as he was in the habit of doing (he and Rhomeo had been shut in there together for almost an hour). After he had heard their confession, Friar Laurens said to Julliette: "My daughter, according to what Rhomeo here has told me, you have agreed to take him as your husband and he likewise agrees to take you as his wife. Are you still of this mind?" The lovers replied that they wished for nothing else. Seeing that they were of the same mind, after having spoken briefly in favour of the dignity of marriage, he pronounced the words required by Church ordinance at marriage ceremonies. Once Julliette had received the ring from Rhomeo, they rose to their feet before the friar who said to them: "If you wish to speak together about private matters, make haste, for I wish to show Rhomeo out without the others knowing." In a hurry to withdraw, Rhomeo whispered to Julliette that she was to send the dame to him after dinner; he would have a rope ladder made by means of which that very evening he would climb through the window into her room where they would decide at greater leisure what they were going to do. This having been decided between them, they both returned home overjoyed, awaiting the happy hour when they would consummate their marriage.

Once home, Rhomeo made known all that had happened between himself and Julliette to a servant of his named Pierre to whom he would have entrusted his life, such was the loyalty he had shown. He asked Pierre to find him with all haste a rope ladder with two strong iron hooks attached to both ends. This he did without any difficulty, because such ladders are very common in Italy.[49] In the evening around five o'clock Julliette made sure to send the dame to Rhomeo who, having seen to what was needed, had the said ladder given to her, begging her to assure Julliette that that very evening when everyone had gone to sleep he would not fail to be at the usual place. Only those who have experienced such things in the past can know how long that day seemed to these ardent lovers, for each minute of the hour for them lasted one thousand years, with the result that if they had been able to command heaven as Joshua did the sun,[50] the earth would soon have been covered with very dark shadows.

When it was time for their meeting, Rhomeo donned the most magnificent clothing that he had and, guided by Fortune, on realising that he was drawing close to the place from which his heart drew life, was so resolute that he nimbly jumped over the garden wall. Having arrived near the window, he caught sight of Julliette who had already put in place her rope ladder to allow him to come up; and so well had the ladies secured the said ladder with the hooks that without any danger he entered Julliette's bedroom which was as bright as day thanks to three torches filled with virgin wax, which Julliette had had lit so that she could see her Rhomeo better. Julliette's sole adornment was the night cap she was wearing and, as soon as she saw him, she flung her arms around his neck. After having kissed him over and over again countless times, she almost swooned in his arms without having the strength to utter a single word to him. Instead all she could do was sigh, pressing her mouth to Rhomeo's. Thus overcome, she gazed pitifully upon him, which caused him to live and die at one and the same time.

After she had recovered somewhat, sighing from the heart she said to him: "Ah, Rhomeo, model that you are of all virtue and charm, I welcome you to this place where, because of your absence and my fear for you, I have shed so many tears that their source has almost been exhausted. But now that I am holding you in my arms, let death and Fortune do what they will from now on, for the mere favour of your presence more than compensates for all my past woes." With tears in his eyes, Rhomeo replied so as to break his silence: "My lady, although I have never been fortunate enough to make you experience first hand the power that you have over me and the torment I suffer all day long because of you, nevertheless I assure you most sincerely that the most trifling sorrow caused by your absence was a thousand times more painful than death which would have cut my life's thread a long time ago, if I had not been able to hope for this lucky day which, paying me now the just retribution for my past tears, makes me happier than if I ruled the universe. Without indulging any more in recalling our past woes, I beg that henceforth we devote ourselves to appeasing our impassioned hearts. Let us go about our business with such prudence and discretion that our enemies will have no pretext for not letting us live in peace and tranquillity."

Just as Julliette was about to reply, the dame arrived and said to them: "Those who waste time when it is most needed, regain it too late. But since you have caused one another so much suffering, there you have a battlefield that I have laid out for you," she said, showing them the bed that she had made ready. "Take up your arms and henceforth have your revenge while jousting." They readily agreed to this, and then alone together between the sheets, they embraced and exchanged the most tender caresses that love could teach them. Thereafter Rhomeo, breaking the holy bonds of virginity, took possession of that place which had not hitherto been besieged; this he did with such joy and contentment as those who have experienced such pleasures can judge. With their marriage thus consummated, Rhomeo, spurred on by day's importunate arrival, took leave of her vowing to return there without fail every second day by the same means and at a similar time, until Fortune offered them a safe opportunity to disclose their marriage to everyone without fear.

Thus to their boundless satisfaction, their pleasure continued for a month or two until Fortune, envious of their happiness, turned her wheel in order to make them tumble into such an abyss that they repaid her for their borrowed pleasures with a most cruel and pitiable death, as you will hear in what follows hereafter.

Now as we have already specified earlier, the lord of Verona had been unable to reconcile the Capellets and Montesches well enough for there not to remain still sparks of their former enmity, and both sides were awaiting only some slight pretext to set upon each other; which they did. As bloodthirsty men are often wont to commit evil deeds following holy festivities, so during the Easter celebrations a group of Capellets came upon several Montesches near the Borsari gate in the vicinity of the old Verona castle, and without further ado began to fight with them. The Capellets had as the leader of their glorious enterprise a young man in good fettle and skilled in the use of arms, Julliette's first cousin Thibault, who urged his companions to humiliate the Montesches so thoroughly on this outing that they would never forget it.

The uproar increased to such an extent throughout all Verona that help turned up on all sides. When this came to the attention of Rhomeo, who was strolling around the city with some companions of his, he made with all haste for where his relatives and allies were being slaughtered; and having realised that there were several wounded on both sides, he said to his companions: "My friends, let us separate them, for they are fighting together so desperately that they will tear one another to pieces before the game is over." And having said this, he rushed headlong into the middle of the throng where he did nothing but ward off blows from his own relatives as well as from others, shouting loudly at them: "My friends, that is enough! It is time now that our quarrels stopped, for besides the fact that God is greatly offended by them, we are in disgrace with everyone and we are disrupting this principality." But they were so set against one another that they paid no heed to Rhomeo and thought only of killing, dismembering and tearing one another to pieces. The fight between them was so fierce and raging that those who were looking on took fright at seeing them suffer so much, for the ground was all covered with arms, legs, thighs and blood, yet they gave no sign of cowardice.

They continued like that for a long time without it being possible to judge who had the upper hand until Thibault, Julliette's cousin, burning with rage and wrath, turning towards Rhomeo thrust his sword at him, thinking to run him through. But Rhomeo was protected from the blow by the coat of mail that he wore as a rule because of his mistrust of the Capellets. Rhomeo responded by saying to him: "Thibault, you can see from the patience that I have had up until now that I did not come here to kill you or yours, but rather to bring about peace between us, and if you were to think that I had failed in my duty out of lack of courage, you would do great wrong to my reputation. But I beg you to believe that there is another specific consideration that has so influenced me up until now that I have controlled myself, as you can see. I beseech you not to take advantage of this, but rather be content with all the blood that has been spilt and with all the murders committed in the past, without forcing me to do what I do not want to do." "Ah, traitor!" replied Thibault. "You think you can save yourself with the blade of your tongue, but see to defending yourself, for I am about to show you that your tongue cannot protect or shield you well enough to prevent me from taking your life." And thus saying, he dealt him a blow of such fury that, if Rhomeo had not warded it off, Thibault would have severed his head from his shoulders.

But his would-be victim straightaway gave tit for tat, for being indignant not only because of the blow that he had received from Thibault but also because of his insult, Rhomeo began to pursue his enemy with such energy that with the third lunge of his sword he struck him to the ground dead with a thrust to the throat such that he ran it through. This caused the fight to cease, for Thibault, besides being the leader of his group, was a member of one of the foremost families in the city. It was for this reason that the *podestà*[51] had some soldiers assembled with all possible haste to imprison Rhomeo who, seeing the predicament he was in, made his way in secret towards the Church of St Francis and Friar Laurens who, having heard what had happened to him, kept him hidden within the convent until such time as Fortune ordained otherwise.

Once word of the disaster that had befallen Lord Thibault had spread throughout the city the Capellets, dressed in mourning, had the body brought before the lord of Verona, as much to move him to pity as to demand justice of him. The Montesches were also there, pointing out Rhomeo's innocence and Thibault's unprovoked assault. After the council had assembled and witnesses on both sides had been heard, the said lord issued a strict order that they lay down their arms; and where Rhomeo's crime was concerned, because he had killed Thibault in self-defence, he was to be banished for life from Verona.

When this shared misfortune became generally known throughout the city, everyone gave voice to grief and protests. Some lamented the death of Lord Thibault, as much for his skill in arms as for the promise he had shown and the great wealth which would have been his had such a cruel death not forestalled it. Others (the ladies in particular) expressed their grief over the downfall of young Rhomeo who, besides the beauty and becoming manners with which he was endowed, possessed as well an undefinable, innate charm thanks to which he was so loved that all, but above all the hapless Julliette, lamented the disaster that had befallen him.

When informed both of the death of her cousin Thibault and of her husband's banishment, Julliette made the air ring with her interminable, bitter weeping and wretched laments. Then, overwhelmed by the violence of her emotions, she retired to her room and, giving way to her grief, she threw herself on her bed where her sorrow intensified in such an extraordinary manner that she would have moved even the most steadfast to pity. Then looking around wildly as though carried away and noticing by chance the window through which Rhomeo was wont to enter her room, she burst out: "Oh, wretched window, by means of which the bitter course of my first misfortunes was planned! If thanks to you I have hitherto enjoyed some slight pleasure or passing contentment, you are now making me pay such a high price for it that my defenceless body, being able to bear it no longer, will now open life's door so that my spirit, relieved of this mortal burden, may henceforth seek more certain peace elsewhere. Ah, Rhomeo, Rhomeo! When first my intimacy with you began and I listened to your alluring promises backed up with so many solemn oaths, I would never have believed that instead of continuing our love and making peace with my relatives, you would have sought the opportunity to break it with such a cowardly, reprehensible act that your good name would be for ever compromised by it and I, wretch that I am, would lose my consort and husband. But if you were so thirsty for Capellet blood, why did you spare mine, when so often and in private you have had me at the mercy of your cruel hands? Did not your victory over me seem glorious enough without your crowning it with the blood of the dearest of all my cousins? Begone with you, and from now on deceive others, wretched like myself, without ever showing your face before me again or letting any of your excuses fall on my ears. In the meantime I shall shed so many tears as I lament the rest of my sorrowful life that my drained body will soon seek solace in the earth."

Once she had finished what she had to say, her heart so tightened that, unable to weep or speak, she remained so motionless that she appeared transfixed. Then having recovered a little, she said in a weak voice: "Ah, slanderous tongue! How dare you offend someone whom even his enemies praise? How is it that you lay blame on Rhomeo when all agree that he is innocent? What sanctuary will he have from now on, since she who was supposed to be the sole bastion and unshakeable defence against his misfortunes, pursues and maligns him? Let me, therefore, let me make atonement to you for my ingratitude by sacrificing my own life; and by this means the offence that I have committed against your loyalty will be revealed, you will be avenged, and I punished." And as she was trying to say more, all her vital signs became so weak that she appeared close to death.

But the good dame, unable to imagine what was causing Julliette's long absence, suddenly suspected that she was in the grip of some strong emotion and she looked for her at such length throughout all her father's palace that she eventually found her in her room, stretched out on her bed in a swoon, with her hands and feet as cold as marble. Thinking her dead, however, the dame began crying out as though carried away by grief, saying: "Ah, dear child! How your death now grieves me!" And as she was feeling all over her body, she realised that there remained in her a few sparks of life. For this reason she was able to bring her out of her trance, having called her name several times. Then she said to her: "My lady Julliette, I know not what gave rise to this behaviour of yours or to your inordinate sadness, but well can I assure you that for this past hour I have been thinking about going to the grave with you." "Alas, dear love," replied the disconsolate Julliette, "can you not see why I am rightly grieving and lamenting, having lost at one and the same time the two people who were most dear to me in all the world?" "It seems to me," the good woman replied, "that because of your reputation it ill becomes you to take it so hard, for the time when wisdom is most called for is when trouble occurs. And now that Lord Thibault is dead, do you think you can bring him back with your tears? What can be held responsible for his death, if not his excessive presumption and recklessness? Would you have wanted Rhomeo to wrong himself and his entire family by allowing himself to be insulted by someone to whom he was not inferior in any way? Be satisfied that Rhomeo is alive, and such is the state of affairs he is in that with time he can be recalled from his exile, for he is a great lord, as you know, well connected and well loved by all. Therefore you must arm yourself with patience from now onwards, for although Fortune may separate you from him for a time, nevertheless I am certain that she will restore him to you later, giving rise to greater joy and contentment than you have yet known. And so that we may be more confident about how he is, I shall find out today from Friar Laurens where he has gone, if you will promise me you will no longer give way to sadness in this way."

Julliette agreed to this, and the good dame then took the direct road to the Church of St Francis where she found Friar Laurens, who informed her that Rhomeo would visit Julliette without fail that evening at the usual time, and would let her know what his plans were for the future. That day thus went by as days do for sailors who, after having been tossed around by violent storms, take heart on seeing a few rays of sunlight break through the sky to light up the earth; and while they imagine they have avoided being shipwrecked, immediately afterwards the sea chances to swell and the waves to pound with such force that the sailors are plunged back into even greater danger than that in which they had previously been.

When it was time for their rendezvous Rhomeo, true to his promise, made for the garden where he found ready the equipment he needed to climb into Julliette's bedroom. With her arms open in welcome, she began to embrace him so tightly that it seemed his soul might depart his body. They both remained thus grief-stricken a good quarter hour, unable to utter a single word; and with their faces pressed closely together, their kisses mingled with the copious tears falling from their eyes. Noticing this Rhomeo said, thinking to calm her a little: "My love, I do not intend at this time to recount to you in detail the variety of strange events wrought by fickle, unstable Fortune that raises man in a trice to the highest point of her wheel, and yet in less than a twinkling of an eye she humbles and humiliates him so thoroughly that in one day she concocts more woes for him than she does favours in one hundred years. This is what is now being demonstrated in my case: I who have been tenderly raised in the midst of my family and have lived in prosperity and grandeur such as you, too, have known, hoped to crown my happiness by reconciling your relatives and mine with our marriage and then living out the life span that God has ordained for me. Nevertheless all my ventures have been thwarted and my plans upset, with the result that from now on I shall have to go wandering in strange parts far from my own people, without any safe haven to which I can retreat. I wanted to tell you all this so as to beg you in the future to bear with patience both my absence and whatever God wills for you."

But Julliette, completely given over to tears and mortal anguish, would not let him continue but rather said, interrupting him: "Rhomeo, how could you be so hard-hearted and pitiless as to think of leaving me here alone, beset by so many deadly woes? At no time of day is death not with me but so unfortunate am I that I still do not die. Thus it would truly seem that death wants to spare my life so as to delight in my suffering and gloat over my misfortune; and as minister and instrument of death's cruelty, you have no scruples that I can see about abandoning me now that you have plucked the flower of my virginity. From this I conclude that all the laws of love are dead and buried, since he who gave me more reason than any other to hope and for whom I have become my own enemy, scorns and despises me. No, no, Rhomeo. You must accept one of two things: either that I follow you forthwith by plunging from the window's heights, or that you allow me to accompany you wherever Fortune leads you, for my heart has become so much a part of yours that when I learn of your departure, I at once feel my life slipping away from me, for I have no desire to go on living other than to delight in your presence and share equally in all your misfortunes. Thus I beg you in all humility, Rhomeo, if ever pity was to be found in the heart of a nobleman, that it now find a place in yours and that you accept me as your servant and faithful companion in your troubles. And should you find it unfitting that I go dressed as a woman, who is to prevent me changing my clothing? Will I be the first woman to have done so in order to escape the tyranny of her family? Do you fear that my service will not be as acceptable as that of Pierre, your servant? Will my loyalty fall short of his? Does not my beauty, which at other times you have praised so highly, have any power over you? My tears, my love and the past pleasures that you have had from me, are they to be cast into oblivion?"

Seeing that Julliette was becoming upset and fearing that she might become even more so, Rhomeo took her into his arms straightaway and, kissing her lovingly, said: "Julliette, sole mistress of my heart, I beg you in the name of God and the fervent love that you bear me, that you entirely eradicate all such thoughts if you do not seek to ruin completely your own life and mine as well, for this will surely come to pass if you act on your intentions. When your absence is made known, your father will have us pursued so hotly that we cannot avoid being discovered, caught, and finally punished most cruelly, me as your abductor and you as a disobedient daughter; and thus, while we were thinking to live happily, our days will be ended by a shameful death. But if you will take heart and be guided by reason rather than by the pleasure that we could give one another, I shall see to it that within three or four months at the most I shall be recalled from exile. And should it be ordained otherwise, I shall return to you come what may and, backed by my friends, I shall take you away from Verona by force, and definitely not disguised as a foreigner but as my wife and companion for life. Thus you must curb your emotions from now on and live secure in the knowledge that death alone can separate me from you, and nothing else."

Rhomeo's reasoning was so convincing that Julliette replied: "My love, I want only what pleases you. Thus it is that, wherever you go, my heart will remain with you as a pledge of the power that you have given me over you. In the meanwhile, I beg that without fail you have Friar Laurens pass on to me frequent news both of the state of our affairs and of your whereabouts." So these two unfortunate lovers spent the night together until daybreak forced them to part, to their extreme sorrow and unhappiness.

Having taken leave of Julliette, Rhomeo made his way to the Church of St Francis and after he had told Friar Laurens what had befallen him, he left Verona dressed as a foreign merchant. He made such good time that he reached Mantua without incident, accompanied only by his servant Pierre whom he immediately sent back to Verona to his father's service. There he rented a house, and living in honourable company, for a few months he attempted to while away the boredom that tormented him.

But during Rhomeo's absence, the wretched Julliette's attempts at calling a halt to her sorrow were such that her heartache was easily discernible in the poor colour of her countenance. For this reason her mother, hearing her sigh and lament day and night without respite, could not refrain from saying to her: "My dear, if you go on much longer like this you will send your aged father and likewise myself, to whom you are as dear as life, to an early grave. So restrain yourself henceforth and try to be of good cheer, banishing from your thoughts the death of your cousin, Thibault. If it so pleased God to call him, do you think you can bring him back with your tears? Do you think it fit to go against His will?" But the poor girl, unable to hide her pain, replied: "My lady, I shed my last tears for Thibault a long time ago, and I believe their source to be so dried up that no more tears will spring from it." Her mother, who did not know what her daughter was driving at, said no more for fear of upsetting her.

Seeing that Julliette's habitual sadness and anguish were persisting, a few days later her mother endeavoured by all means to learn, both from Julliette herself and from all the servants in the house, the reason for her sorrow; but all was in vain. Thus saddened beyond measure, the poor mother took it upon herself to tell everything to her husband, Lord Antonio. Thus one day when she found him at an opportune time, she said to him: "My lord, if you have given thought to our daughter's countenance and behaviour since the death of her cousin, Lord Thibault, you will have found such a marked change in them that you will be amazed, for not only has she chosen not to eat, drink, and sleep, but she has given herself over entirely to weeping and wailing. Her sole pleasure consists in shutting herself away in her room where she becomes so overwrought that, if we do not take matters in hand, I fear hereafter for her life; and if the cause of her illness remains unknown, it will be more difficult to remedy. You see, although I have gone to great lengths I have been able to learn nothing, and however convinced I was at the beginning that everything stemmed from the death of her cousin, I have now changed my mind. Besides which, she herself assured me that she had shed her last tears for him. Not knowing what to do, I wondered to myself if she was thus despondent because of some secret resentment that she has formed on seeing most of her companions married and herself not, perhaps getting it into her head that we wish her to remain thus. Hence, my dear, for our peace of mind as well as hers, I lovingly beg that hereafter you look to arranging a worthy match for her."

Lord Antonio agreed willingly to this, saying to his wife: "My dear, I had already thought several times about what you are saying;

however, seeing that Julliette had not yet reached eighteen years of age, I decided to take my time in attending to it. Nevertheless, since matters are at such a pass and daughters are a dangerous treasure, I shall attend to it with such dispatch as will satisfy you and restore her state of health, which is visibly deteriorating. Meanwhile, find out if she is in love with someone so that we do not have to give as much consideration to the wealth or importance of the family into which we could marry her, as we do to the life and health of our daughter, who is so dear to me that I would rather die poor and disinherited than give her to someone who mistreated her."

A few days after Lord Antonio had broached the question of his daughter's marriage, several noblemen came to him asking to marry her, as much for her unsurpassed beauty as for her wealth and lineage. But out of all of them, an alliance with Paris, the young Count of Lodrone, seemed the most advantageous to Lord Antonio; to him he betrothed her willingly, but after letting his wife know of it. Overjoyed that such an honourable match had been found for her daughter, she had her summoned in private and explained to her what had transpired between her father and Count Paris, emphasising this young count's good looks and charm, attributes for which he was commended by everyone, and she concluded by mentioning the great wealth and endowments with which Fortune had favoured him, by means of which she and her kin would live in everlasting honour.

But Julliette, who would sooner have consented to being dismembered alive than agree to this marriage, said to her mother with unwonted boldness: "My lady, I am amazed that you should have been so free with your daughter as to entrust her to the will of someone else without first consulting her. You will do just as you think best; but be assured that if you do, it will be against my will. And where Count Paris is concerned, I shall lose my life before he shares my body; so you will be my murderer, having delivered me into the hands of someone whom I neither can nor will nor could ever learn to love. I therefore beg that you let me live from now on without troubling about me, as long as my cruel destiny has otherwise disposed of me."

Julliette's sorrowful mother, confused and beside herself, not knowing what to make of her daughter's reply went and found Lord Antonio to whom she told everything, holding nothing back. Indignant beyond measure, the good old man ordered that she be brought immediately before him, by force if she refused to come of her own will. As soon as she had arrived, weeping, she threw herself at his feet which she drenched with the flood of tears falling from her eyes; and as she was about to open her mouth and beg him for mercy, her sobs and sighs so prevented her from speaking that she remained silent without being able to utter a single word. But the old man, completely unmoved by his daughter's tears, said to her very angrily: "Come now, ungrateful and disobedient daughter, have you already forgotten what you heard so often at my table, of the authority that my ancient Roman forefathers had over their children? Not only were they allowed to sell, pawn, and, if need be, cast them aside just as they pleased, but they even had full power of life and death over them. With what irons, what torments, what bonds would these good fathers punish you if they were restored to life? And what if they saw the ingratitude, disloyalty, and disobedience that you display towards your father who, with many an entreaty and request has provided you with one of the foremost lords in this region, one of the best known for all kinds of outstanding qualities, one of whom you and I are unworthy as much for the great wealth to which he is destined as for the greatness and nobility of the family of which he is born? And yet you are fussy and obstinate, and wish to go against my will. I swear by the power of Him who granted you to me that if, by the end of Tuesday, you fail to make ready to be at my castle at Villafranca where Count Paris is also to betake himself, and if there you fail to give your consent to what your mother and I have already agreed to, not only shall I deprive you of all my worldly possessions, but I shall make you marry such a cramped and grim prison that you will curse a thousand times the day and hour of your birth. See henceforth to doing your duty. For had I not promised you to Count Paris, I would this instant make you realise how mighty is the righteous anger of a father roused to indignation by an ungrateful child." And without waiting for any reply from her, the old man left his daughter on her knees in the room.

Knowing her father's rage and fearing to incur his indignation or provoke him further, Julliette withdrew for the day to her room, where all night long she made use of her eyes more for weeping than for sleeping. In the morning she set off and, pretending she was going to Mass with her chamber lady, she reached the Franciscan friars. After having had Friar Laurens summoned, she begged him to hear her confession. No sooner was she on her knees before him than she began her confession with tears, pointing out to him the great misfortune that was in store for her because of the marriage with Count Paris agreed to by her father. She concluded by saying to him: "Sire, because you know that I cannot be married twice and that I have only one God, one husband, and one faith, on leaving here today I intend ending my woeful life with these two hands that you see joined in front of you, so that my spirit may bear testimony to heaven and my blood to earth that my faith and loyalty have been preserved." Then having finished what she had to say, she glanced around distractedly, giving to understand with her wild expression that she had something sinister in mind. Friar Laurens, astonished beyond measure and fearing that she would carry out what she had planned, said to her: "Julliette, my young lady, I beg you in the name of God, calm down a little and stay here quietly until I have attended to your business, for before you leave this convent I shall give you such solace and shall remedy your sorrows so well that you will be satisfied and content."

Having left her in this positive state of mind, he went out of the church and straight up to his room where he began turning over different things in his mind, feeling now tempted to allow her marriage to Count Paris, while knowing that through his own intervention she had married another; now complicating the venture and making it even more dangerous to execute, especially as he was putting himself in the hands of a young, simple, artless maiden, for if she failed in something, their whole venture would be disclosed, his reputation would be compromised, and her husband, Rhomeo, punished. Yet after being beset by a multitude of thoughts, he was at last won over by pity and decided that he would rather risk his good name than permit Paris' adultery with Julliette. Having decided this, he opened his closet, took out a phial, and returned to Julliette, whom he found benumbed, awaiting news that would mean her life or death.

The friar asked: "Julliette, for when has your wedding been arranged?" "The first meeting," she replied, "is Wednesday, the day arranged for me to give my consent to the marriage granted by my father to Count Paris; the marriage celebrations, however, are not to take place until the tenth day of September." "My daughter," said the friar, "take heart. The Lord has shown me a way to deliver you and Rhomeo from the servitude lying in store for you. I have known your husband from the cradle. He has always entrusted me with his most intimate secrets, and I love him as dearly as if he were my own son. For this reason my heart could not suffer that wrong be done to him in any matter that could be put right with my counsel; and especially as you are his wife, I must likewise love you and do my utmost to deliver you from the torment and anguish so beleaguering you. Listen, then, my daughter, to the secret that I am now going to reveal, and above all take care not to make it known to a living soul, for it means life and death to you."

"As you very well know from what is widely reported among the citizens of this city and from what is reputed everywhere about me, I have covered almost all inhabited regions in my travels, with the result that over a period of twenty continuous years I have allowed my body no rest, but instead I exposed it more often than not to the mercy of the brute beasts of the deserts and sometimes to the mercy of the sea, of pirates, and of a thousand other dangers and shipwrecks to be found both on land and sea. Now the fact is, my daughter, that all my wandering has by no means been useless, for besides the incredible personal satisfaction that I usually derive from it, I have as well reaped another particular fruit which, with the grace of God, you will shortly come to know."

"I have, you see, learned of the secret properties of stones, plants, metals, and other things hidden in the bowels of the earth. Contrary to ordinary men, I can make use of these things when the necessity arises, particularly in matters which I know cause God less offence. For as you know, being as I am close to the grave and as my hour of reckoning is drawing near, from now on I must be more fearful of God's judgements than I was when the passions of reckless youth surged within my body."

"Understand then, my daughter, that along with the other graces and favours that heaven bestowed upon me, a long time ago I learned how to make a certain compound out of sleep-inducing herbs and I put it to the test; after it has been reduced to a powder and drunk with a little water, within a quarter of an hour it puts whomever takes it into such a deep sleep and so thoroughly shrouds the senses and other vital spirits that no doctor, no matter how expert, would pronounce him who had taken some of it anything but dead. And it has another even more marvellous effect: the person who takes it feels no pain, and according to the size of the dose consumed, the patient remains thus peacefully asleep; then when it has run its course, he returns to his former condition. So listen now to what you must do: cast aside this womanly frame of mind and arm yourself with manly courage, for the future success or failure of this matter depends solely upon the strength of your heart."

"Here," he continued, "is a phial which I am giving you. You must guard it with your life and on the eve of your wedding, or before dawn the morning of the wedding, you will fill it with water and drink the entire contents. You will then feel a pleasant drowsiness which will gradually spread throughout your entire body. Your limbs will become so numb that you will be unable to move them, and by not performing their usual functions, they will lose their natural feeling. You will remain in this trance for at least forty hours, during which time you will have no pulse nor make any perceptible movement. This will amaze those who come to see you and they will pronounce you dead. Thus according to the custom of our city, they will have you brought to the cemetery near our church and they will have you placed in the tomb where your Capellet ancestors have been buried. In the meantime, I shall send a man in all haste to advise Lord Rhomeo of our whole venture. He is in Mantua and will not fail to be at the tomb the following night, when he and I will open the vault and take your body away. Then once the effects of the powder have worn off, he will be able to take you secretly to Mantua unbeknownst to your relatives and friends; perhaps then, once Rhomeo's banishment has been revoked, he will be able to come out of hiding, to the contentment of all your relatives."

When the friar had finished what he had to say, a new joy began to take hold of Julliette's heart; and so attentively had she listened to him that she did not forget a single word he had said. She then said to him: "Father, do not fear that my courage will fail me as I carry out your orders, for even if it were some strong and deadly poison, I would sooner subject my body to it than consent to fall into the hands of him who can have no share in me. With greater reason, then, must I take heart and expose myself to mortal danger so as to be close to him upon whom wholly depend my life and all the contentment that I ask of this world." "Go, then, my daughter, in God's keeping," said the friar. "I shall pray to Him to guide you and strengthen your will as you carry out your work."

After she had left Friar Laurens, Julliette returned around eleven o'clock to her father's stately house where she found her mother waiting for her at the door, very anxious to ask her if she meant to persist in her early folly. But without giving her mother a chance to question her, Julliette, looking more cheerful than usual, said to her: "My lady, I have come from the Church of St Francis where I perhaps remained longer than duty demanded. Nevertheless, it has been to good purpose and has brought great tranquillity to my troubled mind, thanks to our spiritual father, Friar Laurens, to whom I spoke at length about my life, even telling him in confession what had taken place between my lord father and you with regard to my marriage to Count Paris. But the old man was able to win me over so thoroughly with his saintly admonitions and commendable exhortations that although I had no desire ever to be married, I am now prepared to obey you in whatever you see fit to command me. For this reason, my lady, I beseech that you beg my lord and father to pardon me and tell him, if it so pleases you, that in obedience with his order I am ready to go and meet Count Paris at Villafranca and accept him there as my lord and husband in your presence. As a pledge of what I say, I am now going to my room to select my most precious adornments so that I will be more pleasing to him when he sees me so well attired."

So overcome with joy that she could not utter a single word in reply, Julliette's good mother hurried off to find her husband, Lord Antonio, to whom she related in detail her daughter's amenability and how, by means of Friar Laurens, she had completely capitulated. Overjoyed, the good old man praised God in his heart for this, saying: "My dear, this is not the first benefit that we have received from this holy man, just as there is no citizen in this principality who is not beholden to him. Would that it had pleased Lord God that I had bought twenty of his years with a third of my wealth, so grievous is his advanced old age to me."

Lord Antonio went at the same time to find Count Paris with the idea of persuading him to go to Villafranca, but the Count pointed out to him that the expense would be excessive and that it would be better to reserve this expenditure for the wedding day so as to celebrate it with more pomp.[52] Nevertheless, he was in favour of going to see Julliette if Lord Antonio thought it wise, and so they left together to go and meet with her. Advised of the Count's impending arrival, Julliette's mother saw to readying her daughter, whom she ordered to spare none of her charms when the count came.

Julliette used her charms to such good effect that before the count left the house she had so completely stolen his heart that henceforth his life depended on her. He was so anxious for the appointed hour to arrive that he constantly pressed her father and mother for the celebration and consummation of the marriage. And thus this day went by in considerable joy, and several more besides up to the day preceding the wedding, for which Julliette's mother had made full provision as befitted the magnificence and importance of their family.

Villafranca, of which we have already made mention, was a place in the country a mile or two from Verona where Lord Antonio was often wont to go for purposes of recreation. It was here that the wedding banquet was to be prepared, although the requisite ceremony was to take place in Verona. Feeling her hour approaching, Julliette pretended as best she could and when the time came for her to retire, her chamber lady wanted to keep her company and sleep in her room, as she usually did. But Julliette said to her: "My dear friend, as you know tomorrow my marriage is to be celebrated, and as I wish to spend most of the night in prayer, I beg you to leave me by myself for today; come tomorrow about six o'clock to help me dress." The good dame readily agreed to this, not suspecting for a moment what Julliette had in mind to do.

Having retired alone to her room, Julliette filled the phial which the friar had given her with water from a jar on the table, and after having made this mixture she placed everything under the bolster on her bed and then lay down. Once in bed, new thoughts began to beset her along with such a great dread of death that she was at a loss what to do. Lamenting incessantly, she said: "Am I not the most wretched and desperate woman ever born? The world holds nothing for me but misfortune, misery, and mortal sadness, since things have come to such a pass that I must here swallow a draught whose properties are unknown to me, so as to save my honour and my conscience. But what if," she continued, "this powder takes effect sooner or later than is needed? What if I become the talk of the city once my misconduct becomes known? Moreover, what if snakes and other poisonous creatures usually found in tombs and dungeons set upon me, thinking I am dead? But how will I be able to endure the stench of all the decaying flesh and bones of my ancestors who are resting in this vault, if by chance I were to awake before Rhomeo and Friar Laurens came to my aid?"

Just as she was giving herself over to such thoughts, her imagination became so enflamed that she believed she saw some apparition or ghost of her cousin Thibault exactly as he had been when she had seen him wounded and bleeding; and dreading that she had to be buried alive next to him, with so many dead bodies and bones stripped of flesh, her young and delicate body began to shudder with fear and her blond hair to stand on end to the extent that, beset as she was with dread, a cold sweat began to drench her skin and bathe all her limbs with the result that she thought she already had countless dead bodies around her tugging at her from all sides and tearing her to pieces. Feeling that her strength was waning bit by bit and fearing that weakness would prevent her from seeing her undertaking through, without further thought she swallowed the water contained in the phial as though completely out of her mind. Then crossing her arms over her breast, she immediately lost all feeling in her body and fell into a trance.

As dawn was beginning to raise its head over the East, Julliette's chamber lady, who had locked her in with a key, opened the door and, thinking to wake her, called her repeatedly, saying: "My lady, you have overslept! Count Paris will come to get you up." The poor woman's words fell on deaf ears, for even if all the most horrible and clamorous sounds in the world had echoed in Julliette's ears, her vital spirits were so sluggish and dulled that they would not have woken her. Amazed by this, the poor dame began to feel her but found her as cold as marble all over. Then placing her hand over Julliette's mouth, she suddenly concluded that she was dead, as she had found no sign of breathing. As though out of her mind she ran to break the news to Julliette's mother who, as frenzied as a tigress that has lost its cubs, went straight into her daughter's bedroom. Having seen the sorry state she was in, believing her dead she cried out: "Ah, cruel death! You have robbed me of all my joy and happiness! Lest my suffering increase if I am allowed to spend the rest of my days in sadness, scourge me, too, with your fury!" She then began to sigh in such a way that it seemed her heart would break.

Hardly had she begun to cry out more loudly than there appeared Julliette's father, Count Paris, and a large number of noble men and women who had come to honour the marriage celebration with their presence. As soon as they had heard everything, such was their sorrow that whoever then had seen their faces would easily have judged that to be the day of wrath and pity. This was particularly true of Lord Antonio, whose heart was so aching that he could neither weep nor speak. Not knowing what to do, he sent straightaway for the city's most expert doctors who, after having made enquiries about Julliette's past life, were unanimous in their judgement that she had died of melancholy, at which the sorrow began again with renewed vigour.

If ever a day was woeful, piteous, unhappy, and grievous, without doubt it was the day when Julliette's death was heralded throughout Verona, for it was so regretted by young and old alike that it seemed, judging by the general lamentation, that the entire principality was in peril. And not without cause, for besides the unaffected beauty and many virtues with which nature had adorned her, she was so without airs, so wise and good-natured that, because of this humility and courtesy of hers, she had so stolen everyone's heart that there was not one person who did not lament her calamity.

While these things were going on, Friar Laurens dispatched in haste from his convent a friar named Friar Anselme, whom he trusted as he would himself, and gave him a letter written in his own hand, ordering him expressly not to give it to anyone but Rhomeo. In this letter he told of all that had transpired between him and Julliette, pointing out the powder's properties, and he sent word that he was to come the following night because the powder would then cease to work. He was to take Julliette away with him in disguise to Mantua until Fortune ordained otherwise.

The friar made such good speed that he arrived in Mantua shortly after, and since the custom in Italy is that Franciscan friars must take a companion from their order with them when they go about their business in the city, the friar made his way to the Franciscan convent. But after he had entered, he was not permitted to go out again that same day as he had thought to do, because several days earlier a friar in the convent had died, it was said, of plague. For this reason the health officials had forbidden the gate-keeper to allow his friars to go about the city or to be in communication with any of its citizens until the officers of the law had given them permission. This gave rise to great woe, as you will see from what follows.

This friar, finding himself in the predicament of not being able to leave the convent, added to which he did not know what the letter contained, decided to postpone his business for that day. While things were at this pass, preparations for Julliette's funeral were under way in Verona. Now there is the custom, common in Italy, of putting all the most eminent descendants of the one family line in the same tomb, which was why Julliette was put in the Capellet family vault in a cemetery near the Church of the Franciscan Friars, where

Thibault likewise was buried. Once the funeral rites had been carried out with honour, everyone went away.

Pierre, Rhomeo's servant, had been present at the funeral, for (as we have said earlier) his master had sent him back from Mantua to Verona to rejoin his father's service and to advise him of whatever might be plotted during his absence. Having seen Julliette's body shut in the tomb and, like everyone else, believing her dead, he set out with all possible haste. Once in Mantua, he found his master in his usual house and, with his eyes wet with tears, said to him: "My lord, an event so strange has befallen you that I fear being the cruel agent of your death if you do not take heart. I must tell you, my lord, that as of yesterday morning my lady Julliette has departed this world to seek rest in the other; with my own eyes I saw her buried in the cemetery of the Church of St Francis."

On hearing this sad news Rhomeo began to display such sorrow that it seemed as though his spirits, besieged by such emotional torment, would at once flee his body. But overpowering love, which would not allow him to falter till the very end, put it into his head that if he could die close to her, his death would be more glorious and she (or so it seemed to him) would be placated. After washing his face for fear that signs of his grief would be evident, he thus left his room and forbad his servant to follow him. He then searched the whole city to see if he could find a fitting remedy for his woes. Having espied amongst others an apothecary's shop very poorly stocked with boxes and other things necessary to his profession, it thus occurred to Rhomeo that the apothecary's extreme poverty would make him consent willingly to what he meant to ask of him. And after drawing him to one side, he whispered to him: "Master, here are fifty ducats that I am giving you in exchange for a poison so potent that whoever makes use of it dies within a quarter of an hour." Overcome by greed, the wretched fellow agreed to what Rhomeo was asking of him and, pretending in the presence of others to give him some other medicine, he prepared the poison for him straightaway. He then said softly to Rhomeo: "My lord, I am giving you more than you need since just half this amount is all it takes to kill within an hour the most robust man in the world."

After having put his poison in his pouch, Rhomeo returned home where he ordered his servant to set out in haste for Verona; once there he was to secure a supply of candles, steel for the tinder-box, and the tools needed to open Julliette's vault. Rhomeo urged him above all to be sure to wait for him near the cemetery of St Francis and not to mention his calamity to anyone along the way. Pierre was meticulous in carrying out his master's orders, and such was his haste that he arrived early in Verona, where he saw to everything that he had been instructed to do. In the meantime Rhomeo, spurred on by deadly thoughts, had ink and paper brought to him and jotted down a brief account of his love, the wedding between him and Julliette, and how they had consummated it, Friar Laurens' help, his purchase of the poison, and finally, his death. Then having brought his tragic tale to an end, he closed the letters, placed his seal on them, and addressed them to his father; and stowing his letters away in his pouch, he mounted his horse and made such haste that he arrived under cover of night in the city of Verona before the gates had been closed.

Here he found his servant waiting for him with a lantern and the above-mentioned tools needed to open the vault. Rhomeo said to him: "Pierre, help me open this vault, and as soon as it is open, I order you on pain of death not to come near me nor to put any obstacle in the way of anything that I may wish to carry out. Here is a letter that you are to give my father tomorrow morning when he arises; it will perhaps give him more pleasure than you think." Unable to imagine what his master intended to do, Pierre moved back a little so as to study his gestures and expression.

When the tomb was open, Rhomeo went down two steps holding the candle in his hand and glimpsed with piteous eyes the body of her who was his reason for living. Then having bathed her with his tears and kissed her ardently, holding her in his arms, unable to tear his eyes away from her, he placed his fearful hands on Julliette's cold breast. After he had searched various parts of her body in vain for signs of life, he took the poison out of its box and, having swallowed a large amount of it, he exclaimed: "Oh, Julliette, of whom the world was unworthy, what more pleasing death could my heart choose than to die near you? What more glorious burial than to be enclosed in your tomb? What better or more worthy epitaph could be consecrated to memory than this shared and piteous sacrifice of our lives?" And while he was striving to resume his mourning with increased intensity, his heart began trembling due to the virulence of the poison which was gradually taking it over.

Looking here and there, near the body of Julliette Rhomeo espied that of Thibault not yet completely decomposed and, addressing him as though he were alive, said: "Cousin Thibault, wherever you may be I cry out to you now for mercy for the offence I caused you in taking your life, and if you wish to be avenged on me, what greater or more cruel satisfaction could you hereafter hope for than to see him who has harmed you poisoned by his own hand and buried beside you?" Then having finished what he had to say and feeling his life gradually ebbing away, getting to his knees he murmured weakly: "Lord God, who to redeem me came down from your father's bosom and became flesh in the womb of the Virgin, I beg you to have pity on this poor afflicted soul, for well I know that this body is no longer but earth." Then gripped by a desperate pain, he fell onto Julliette's body with such force that his heart, weakened by excessive anguish and no longer able to withstand this last, cruel strain, lost all its natural feeling and functions. Thus his soul immediately departed his body and he was left sprawled out and lifeless.

Friar Laurens, who knew for exactly how long his powder would work, set out from the Church of St Francis, amazed that he had had no reply to the letter he had sent Rhomeo by means of his companion, Friar Anselme; and he was considering opening the tomb with his own tools so as to provide air for Julliette who was about to wake up. Drawing near the place, he caught a glimpse of the light inside which filled him with terror, until Pierre, who was nearby, reassured him that the person within was Rhomeo who had been weeping and wailing incessantly for half an hour. They then entered the vault and finding Rhomeo lifeless, gave themselves over to such sorrow as only those who have truly loved can understand.

Whilst they were thus lamenting, Julliette, noticing the brightness in the tomb as she came out of her trance, did not know if it was a dream or an apparition appearing before her eyes. As she recovered consciousness she recognised Friar Laurens and said to him: "Father, I beg you in God's name, assure me of your promise, for I am completely bewildered." And then speaking openly because he feared being discovered for having tarried there too long, Friar Laurens gave her a precise account of how he had sent Friar Anselme off to Mantua to find Rhomeo, from whom he had had no reply; and how despite everything, he had found Rhomeo dead in the vault. He then showed her Rhomeo's body lying next to hers, begging her, moreover, to bear with patience the misfortune that had occurred and adding that, if it so pleased her, he would take her to some secret nunnery where with time she would be able to ease her sorrow and put her soul at rest.

But the moment Julliette cast her eye on Rhomeo's dead body, she was gripped by such a violent outpouring of tears that, unable to endure the violence of her grief, she gasped uncontrollably, her mouth on his. Then by flinging herself on his body and embracing him tightly, it seemed that with her sighing and sobbing she would restore him to life and revive him. And after having kissed him over and over again, she cried out: "Ah, sweet haven of my thoughts and of all the pleasure that ever I enjoyed! Was your heart truly so steadfast that you chose to be buried here in the arms of your perfect lover? And for my sake you chose to finish your life's course in the bloom of youth when living was supposed to be most dear and delightful to you? How was this tender body able to hold out against the frenzied struggle when death made its appearance? How could your tender and delicate years willingly permit you to shut yourself up in this loathsome, foul place wherein henceforth you will serve as food for worms unworthy of you? Alas! Alas! What need did I have for my sorrows to be renewed, when time and my long patience were supposed to put an end to them once and for all? Ah, poor, wretched creature that I am! While thinking to find a remedy for my love, I have sharpened the knife which has made the cruel wound whose mortal injury I now suffer. Ah, blessed and fortunate tomb, for in centuries to come you will serve as witness to the most perfect union of the two most fortunate lovers who ever existed! To you I bequeath the last sighs and outpouring of her who has been more cruelly subjected than any other to sorrow and death."

Just as she was about to resume her lamentation, Pierre warned Friar Laurens that he could hear a noise near the Citadel, and intimidated by it they moved promptly away, afraid of being caught. Realising she was alone with no one to stop her, Julliette then took Rhomeo in her arms once more and kissed him with such feeling that she appeared more overcome by love than by death. Having drawn out the dagger that Rhomeo had girded at his side, she stabbed herself with it several times through the heart, murmuring in a weak and piteous voice: "Ah, death, who are the end of my misfortune and beginning of my happiness, I welcome you! Fling now your darts fearlessly at me and think not to prolong my life any further lest my spirit toil in finding my Rhomeo's amongst so many dead. And you, my dear lord and faithful husband Rhomeo, if you are still able to hear me, receive her whom you loved so faithfully and who was responsible for your violent death! I willingly offer you my soul so that no one but you may enjoy the love that you had so deservedly won, and so that our spirits, on emerging from this light, may live together for all eternity in the place of everlasting immortality." And having finished what she had to say, she gave up the ghost.

While these things were taking place, the town watchmen happened to be passing nearby and, noticing the light in that tomb, they immediately suspected that necromancers had opened the vault to desecrate the corpses and make use of them in their illicit practices. Curious to learn what was going on, they went into the vault where they found Rhomeo and Julliette with their arms around each other's neck as though some sign of life still remained in them. After having taken their time in examining them, they realised to their astonishment what the situation was, and then searched so thoroughly for those they thought had committed the murder that at last they found Friar Laurens and Pierre, the dead Rhomeo's servant, hidden under a bench. They took them off to prison and notified Lord Della Scala and the judicial authorities of Verona of the misfortune that had occurred, which immediately became public knowledge throughout the whole city. You would have seen then all the citizens with their wives and children leaving their houses to behold the piteous sight. And so that the murder be made public in the presence of all the citizens, the judicial authorities ordered the two bodies raised onto a dais in sight of everyone, just as they had been when they were found in the vault. They further ordered that Pierre and Friar Laurens be questioned in public to prevent people murmuring afterwards or pleading ignorance.

Once this worthy old friar was up on the dais, his white beard wet with tears, the judges ordered him to disclose who the perpetrators of this murder were, considering that at an unseemly hour he had been apprehended near the tomb with tools in his possession. Unperturbed by the accusation put forward, Friar Laurens, a straightforward, articulate man, spoke thus to them in a confident voice: "My lords, if you take into account my past life, advanced years, and the sorry spectacle to which I have now been reduced by misfortune, there is not one amongst you who will not be amazed by such a sudden and unexpected change, considering that in the seventy or so years since I came into this world and began to experience its conceits, I have never been accused—and far less convicted—of any crime of which I was ashamed, although before God I acknowledge that I am the greatest and most loathsome sinner in the flock.

Nevertheless, now that I am more prepared for my day of reckoning, now that worms, the earth, and death summon me constantly to face divine justice, now that I do nothing but long for my tomb, it is precisely at this time, or so you are convinced, that I have most compromised and jeopardised my honour and life. And it is perhaps these abundant tears pouring down my face that have induced you to think so badly of me. As if in the Holy Scriptures we do not read of how Jesus Christ wept, moved with human pity and compassion! Moreover, tears are more often than not reliable harbingers of men's innocence. Or rather—and this is more likely—it is the questionable hour and the tools, as the judge has proposed, which make me guilty of the murders, as if the hours had not all been created equal by the Lord. There are twelve of them in a day, just as he himself has pointed out, indicating by this that all minutes and all hours are the same when it comes to doing good or bad deeds, according to whether God's spirit guides or forsakes the person."

"As for the tools that were in my possession when I was apprehended, now is not the time for me to inform you of the purpose for which iron was created in the first place, nor of how by itself it is incapable of increasing good or evil in men, except through the evil intention of him who abuses it. My reason for explaining this is to make you understand that neither my tears, nor the iron tools, nor the questionable hour can convict me of murder or make me other than I am. Only the testimony of my own conscience can do this, for if I were guilty it alone would serve as my prosecutor, witness, and executioner. In view of my age, the repute in which you have held me in the past, and the short time left to me in this world, my conscience ought to trouble me more than all possible mortal punishment could. But thanks be to God, I feel no worm gnawing at me, no remorse pricking me over an event that has left you all shaken and terrified before my eyes. In order to put your souls at rest and allay any qualms which could henceforth trouble your conscience, I swear to you on that part of heaven to which I lay claim that I will now let you hear from beginning to end this sorry tragedy. You will perhaps be no less amazed than these two poor ardent lovers were strong and forbearing in exposing themselves to merciful death because of the fervent and indissoluble love which they bore one another."

The friar then began to tell his listeners of the beginning of Rhomeo and Julliette's love, confirmed over a period of time, after which there ensued the verbal marriage agreement, without the friar's having known anything about it. He spoke of how the lovers, feeling themselves spurred on by a more fervent love, had appealed to him a few days later under the veil of confession, both of them swearing solemnly that they were married and that, if he did not see fit to celebrate their marriage before the Church, they would be forced to offend God and live in sin. In view of this and considering also the alliance to be good as both parties were equal in prestige, wealth, and nobility, he had bestowed his blessing upon them in a chapel, hoping in this way possibly to reconcile the Montesches and Capellets and to perform a deed that would find favour in God's eyes. After this they had consummated their marriage that same night in the Capellet palace, to which Julliette's chambermaid could further testify.

He then mentioned the murder of Thibault, Julliette's cousin, from which there had ensued Rhomeo's banishment. He spoke of how, with Rhomeo gone and their marriage a secret known only to them, steps had been taken to marry her to Count Paris. This had provoked Julliette to throw herself at his feet in a chapel of the Church of St Francis, determined to kill herself if he did not advise her over the marriage with Count Paris agreed to by her father. He concluded by saying that, although old age and the fear of death had made him resolve to repudiate all the occult sciences in which he had indulged in his younger years, nevertheless, pressed by the urgency of her request and by pity and fearing that Julliette would do violence to herself, he had bent his moral principles, preferring to blemish his soul rather than allow this young woman to take her own life, thereby placing her soul in jeopardy. Consequently he had made use of his former guile and had given her a certain sleeping powder because of which she had been pronounced dead.

He then told them how he had sent Friar Anselme to Rhomeo with a letter, advising him of the whole venture, but had not as yet received any reply from him. He then described exactly how he had found Rhomeo dead in the tomb, where in all likelihood he had poisoned or suffocated himself, so grief-stricken had he understandably been on finding Julliette in that state and believing her dead. He then went on to tell them of how Julliette had killed herself with Rhomeo's dagger so as to be with him after death, and how they had been unable to save her because of the noise made by the guards which had forced them to move to one side. And for verification of what he was saying, he beseeched the lord of Verona and the magistrates to send to Mantua to have Friar Anselme brought back so as to learn the cause of his delay; to read the letters that he had sent to Rhomeo; to have both Julliette's lady-in-waiting and Rhomeo's servant, Pierre, questioned. Without waiting for his turn to be interrogated, the latter said to them: "My lords, just as Rhomeo was about to enter the tomb, he handed me these letters, I believe written by him, which he ordered me expressly to give to his father."

When the letters were opened, they were found to contain the entire story, even the name of the apothecary who had sold him the poison, its cost, and the reason why he had used it. Everything was cleared up so well that only an eye witness account of the story could have verified it better. Indeed, everything had been disclosed so systematically that nobody entertained any doubts about it. After he had acquainted the magistrates with all the facts, Bartolomeo della Scala, who was lord of Verona at that time, decided that Julliette's lady-in-waiting should be banished for having kept this clandestine marriage hidden from Rhomeo's father, for if it had been revealed at the right time, a great deal of good would have resulted from it. Pierre, because he had obeyed his master, was set free once more. The apothecary was seized, tortured, convicted, and then hanged. Worthy old Friar Laurens was left in peace with his reputation unblemished, as much out of regard for his past services to the principality of Verona as for his well-earned reputation for probity. He nevertheless shut himself up of his own accord in a small hermitage two miles from Verona, where he lived a further five or six years in constant prayer until he was summoned from this world into the next. And moved to pity by such unparalleled misfortune, the Montesches and Capellets shed such abundant tears that they were purged of their wrath and were thus reconciled from then onwards.

Thus it was that those whom prudence or human counsel had been unable to subdue, were at last conquered and won over by pity. And in order to immortalise the memory of such a perfect and ideal love, the lord of Verona ordered that the bodies of these two wretched lovers remain in the tomb wherein they had ended their lives. This tomb was then set up on a lofty marble column and inscribed with countless unsurpassable epitaphs. And it still exists to this day, so that of all the most exceptional and unique features to be found in the city of Verona, the most famous of all to be seen is the monument of Rhomeo and Julliette.

# *Notes*

1. Masuccio's plot summary differs from the tale in that Ganozza, after learning of Mariotto's hanging, is admitted to a convent where she dies soon after of grief. Olin H. Moore argues that this discrepancy is due to the fact that Masuccio's novella derives from two different sources: Boccaccio's *Decameron* (10,4) and the popular fifteenth-century novella "Istorietta amorosa fra Leonora de' Bardi e Ippolito Buondelmonti." See Olin H. Moore, *The Legend of Romeo and Juliet* (Columbus: Ohio State UP, 1950) 39.
2. Antonio Piccolomini, a nephew of Pius II, became Duke of Amalfi in 1461.
3. The *podestà*, an important transitional figure in Italy in the evolution from republic to *signoria*, was an independent arbitrator to whom the government of the city was handed over for a fixed term so that he could restore peace and order; as the highest judge in the commune, he was required to preside over contentious cases.
4. The Italian expression used here ("san Ioanni Boccadoro") involves an ironic play on words. Masuccio borrows the expression from Boccaccio (*Decameron* 1,6) who conflates the names of two saints (St John the Baptist and St John Chrysostom 349-407) in order to suggest the cupidity of his inquisitor. "Boccadoro" [Goldenmouth] is Boccaccio's translation of the Greek *chrusostomos*, and the face of St John the Baptist appeared on gold florins.
5. Porto Pisano is today known as Livorno (Leghorn); Aigues Mortes is a fortified medieval city defending the mouth of the Rhone.
6. This particular form of punishment or torture ("tratti di corda" or "strappado") consisted in hoisting the subject up by a rope then letting him fall its full length.
7. Bartolomeo dalla Scala (also referred to as Bartolomeo della Scala—the form we will prefer here—and Bartolomeo Scala) was lord of Verona from 1301 to 1304.

8. Da Porto is here referring to the war of the League of Cambrai (1508-1511); see Introduction, note 1. As captain of the Venetian light cavalrymen, Da Porto was badly wounded in 1511.
9. Da Porto refrains from naming Messer Antonio's daughter until the father reveals to her the wedding arrangements he has undertaken on her behalf.
10. In this dance, common in the sixteenth century, the person in whose hands the torch ended up, extinguished it, thus bringing the festivities to a close.
11. It was not uncommon at the time for members of the Church to practise alchemy and magic as well as more orthodox intellectual pursuits.
12. Even without the presence of the friar, Romeo and Giulietta could have wed clandestinely simply by exchanging vows. Only after the Council of Trent (1545-1563) were clandestine marriages of this sort no longer allowed.
13. Giulietta's birthday falls on 16 September. The couple thus met and fell in love the winter following Giulietta's eighteenth birthday.
14. Whereas Madonna Giovanna had earlier used the formal "you"(*voi*) when addressing her husband, both parents use the informal *tu* when speaking to their daughter. Giulietta shows her respect by using the formal *voi* with her parents.
15. The word used here by Frate Lorenzo is *peccato*, which also means "sin". Given, however, that the friar adduces Giulietta's youth and beauty as reasons why she should not take her own life, "pity" is more in keeping with his secular way of thinking in this context.
16. It is only at this stage, when Romeo believes Giulietta to be dead, that he addresses her with the familiar *tu*.
17. A fortified area of the city where the city lord's palace was located; see fig. 1, p. 12.
18. A kind of lantern that can be closed to conceal both the light and the bearer.
19. Pygmalion, a mythical king of Cyprus, fell in love with a statue that he himself had sculpted and he convinced Aphrodite to bring it to life.
20. See note 3 above.
21. Members of the clergy could not be arrested without the permission of the ecclesiastical authorities.
22. Girolamo Fracastoro (1478-1553) was a doctor of such renown that Paul III appointed him doctor of the Council of Trent (1545-1563). Of his many writings the most famous in verse is a poem in Latin on syphilis ("Syphilis sive de Morbo gallico", Verona, 1530).

23. In 1529 Bandello entered the service of Cesare Fregoso, exiled captain of Francis I, who remained Bandello's patron until Fregoso's assassination in 1541.
24. A small city near Verona important for its thermal waters.
25. See note 7 above.
26. Fracastoro's epigram ("In Bandelli Parcas ad Ianum Caesaris Fregosi filium") was written in response to Bandello's composition *Le tre Parche* celebrating the birth of Giano Fregoso.
27. The narrator here is the Veronese Alessandro Peregrino; Bandello, on the other hand, was born in Castelnuovo Scrivia, which today belongs to the province of Alessandria in Piedmont.
28. See note 10 above.
29. Unlike her counterpart in Da Porto's novella, Madonna Giovanna addresses her husband familiarly and is similarly addressed by him in return. This is in keeping with the general lowering of the tone in Bandello's version, discernible from the beginning with the frame setting's abandonment of chivalry in favour of a more mundane tone.
30. Cf. note 13 above.
31. Celebrated on 15 August.
32. Giulietta here engages in a play on words, calling the Count of Lodrone a thief (*ladrone* in Italian) as he wishes to 'steal' what belongs to Romeo.
33. According to medieval physiology, the human body was comprised of four humours (blood, phlegm, and black and yellow bile) which, by their relative proportions, determined the individual's state of health and temperament.
34. Galen (circa 130-200 A.D.), after Hippocrates, the most distinguished physician of antiquity; Hippocrates (400 B.C.), Greek physician, traditionally regarded as the "father of medicine"; Johannes Mesuë the Elder (776-855 A.D.), an Arab Christian who, early in the ninth century, became a hospital director at Baghdad, which became one of the world's important medical centres; Avicenna (980-1037 A.D.), a Persian philosopher and physician.
35. Here as elsewhere in the tale, the narrating voice intervenes to comment on the fatality which directs the events to their tragic conclusion.
36. See note 18 above.
37. The expression here used by Romeo (*l'acqua del serpe*) in referring to the poison means literally "serpent water". From what Romeo says shortly afterwards about how he procured it, it would appear that he drank snake venom.

38. Bandello, like Da Porto before him, has Giulietta address Romeo with the familiar "you" (*tu*) only after he dies.
39. According to medieval physiology, the spirits were fluids within the human body that determined its vital functions.
40. See note 3 above.
41. Rather than summarise the story that he is about to relate, Boaistuau instead touches on the theme of the fatality of ardent love, as though this (rather than external obstacles such as the enmity between the Montesches and the Capellets) were directly responsible for the death of Rhomeo and Julliette. In common with his three Italian predecessors, Boaistuau insists on the historicity of his tale; apart from a vague reference to "some famous Italian or Latin historian", he does not here acknowledge his Italian sources. However, on the title page of the original edition of the *Histoires tragiques* (Paris: Vincent Sertenas, 1559), it is specified that Boaistuau's tales derive from the "oeuvres italiennes de Bandel" ("Italian works of Bandello"); on the title page of the edition which Boaistuau dedicated to Queen Elizabeth I (also 1559) he acknowledges only vaguely "some famous Italian and Latin authors" as his source.
42. Pliny the Elder (23-79 A.D.), a learned Roman, author of the celebrated *Natural History*; Valerius Flaccus (1st century A.D.), a Latin epic poet, author of an *Argonautica*; Plutarch (circa 46-120 A.D.), a Greek biographer and philosopher, famous principally for his *Parallel Lives*..
43. Boaistuau appears to have copied Bandello's title without taking into account the fact that in his own adaptation of the story he introduces the innovation of Julliette dying not of grief but from the stab wounds she inflicts with Rhomeo's dagger. It is noteworthy also that Boaistuau dispenses with the introductory frame setting in which Da Porto and Bandello claim to have first heard the story, which they then record in written form. Boaistuau instead begins directly with the encomium of Verona and the surrounding countryside, present also in Bandello.
44. See note 7 above.
45. The head of the Capellet family is hereafter referred to as Antonio.
46. These parenthetical comments are no less frequent in Boaistuau's version of the tale than they are in Bandello's. As will be seen further on, the French author occasionally intervenes to offer his views on particular aspects of contemporary life or customs. See also Boaistuau, note 49.
47. See note 10 above.
48. Boaistuau's Marcucio is distinguished from his forerunners by his social graces and audacity with women. As his demeaning nick-

name (*Guercio*/Squint-Eyed) has been supressed in this version of the tale, only his icy hands mar the otherwise positive image of the urbane courtier.

49. Although Boaistuau generally adheres closely to Bandello's version of the tale, he occasionally allows himself, as here, to comment with mild disparagement on some detail of the narrative.

50. After Joshua had assumed leadership of the Israelite tribes following the death of Moses, the Amorite kings attacked the city of Gibeon for its defection to the Israelites. Joshua, however, came to the aid of his allies and, by means of a hailstorm and a miraculous extension of the daylight, routed the Amorites. Joshua gives his name to the sixth book of the Old Testament.

51. See note 3 above.

52. Count Paris' pragmatism, original to Boaistuau, is in keeping also with the materialistic mentality of Julliette's parents, who regard their only child as a "dangerous treasure" to be disposed of promptly and honourably.

## Publications of the Centre for Reformation and Renaissance Studies

### Renaissance and Reformation Texts in Translation:

Lorenzo Valla. *The Profession of the Religious and Selections from The Falsely-Believed and Forged Donation of Constantine*. Trans. O.Z. Pugliese. 3rd ed. (1998), pp. 114.

Giovanni Della Casa. *Galateo: A Renaissance Treatise on Manners.* Trans. K. Eisenbichler and K.R. Bartlett. 3rd ed. (1994), pp. 98.

Bernardino Ochino. *Seven Dialogues.* Trans. R. Belladonna (1998), pp. 96.

Nicholas of Cusa. *The Layman on Wisdom and The Mind.* Trans. M.L. Führer (1989), pp. 112.

Andreas Karlstadt, Hieronymous Emser, Johannes Eck. *A Reformation Debate: Karlstadt, Emser, and Eck on Sacred Images.* Trans. B. Mangrum and G. Scavizzi (1998), pp. 115.

*Whether Secular Government Has the Right to Wield the Sword in Matters of Faith. A Controversy in Nürnberg in 1530.* Trans. James M. Estes (1994), pp. 118.

Jean Bodin. *On the Demon-Mania of Witches.* Abridged, trans. & ed. R.A. Scott and J.L. Pearl (1995), pp. 219.

### Tudor and Stuart Texts:

James I. *The True Law of Free Monarchies and Basilikon Doron.* Ed. with an intro. by D. Fischlin and M. Fortier (1996), pp. 181.

*The Trial of Nicholas Throckmorton.* A modernized edition. Ed. with an intro. by Annabel Patterson (1998), pp. 108.

*Early Stuart Pastoral.* The Shepherd's Pipe *by William Browne and others and* The Shepherd's Hunting *by George Wither.* Ed. by James Doelman (1999), pp. 196.

### Occasional Publications:

*Register of Sermons Preached at Paul's Cross 1534–1642.* Comp. M. MacLure. Revised by P. Pauls and J.C. Boswell (1989), pp. 151.

*Annotated Catalogue of Early Editions of Erasmus at the Centre for Reformation and Renaissance Studies, Toronto.* Comp. J. Glomski and E. Rummel (1994), pp. 153.